THE McKINSEY MIND

THE McKINSEY MIND

Understanding and Implementing the Problem-Solving Tools and Management Techniques of the World's Top Strategic Consulting Firm

ETHAN M. RASIEL
AUTHOR OF *THE McKINSEY WAY*
AND PAUL N. FRIGA

McGraw Hill Education (India) Private Limited
CHENNAI

McGraw Hill Education Offices
Chennai New York St Louis San Francisco Auckland Bogotá Caracas
Kuala Lumpur Lisbon London Madrid Mexico City Milan Montreal
San Juan Santiago Singapore Sydney Tokyo Toronto

McGraw Hill Education (India) Private Limited

McGraw Hill Education (India) Edition 2003

24th reprint 2018
RLZYYRYERABRL

Reprinted in India by arrangement with McGraw-Hill Global Education Holdings, LLC, New York

Sales territories: India, Pakistan, Nepal, Bangladesh, Sri Lanka and Bhutan

Library of Congress Cataloging-in-Publication Data

Rasiel, Ethan M.
The McKinsey mind: understanding and implementing the problem-solving tools and management techniques of the world's top strategic consulting firm / Ethan M. Rasiel and Paul N. Friga.
p. cm.
Includes bibliographical references and index
ISBN 0-07-137429-9
1. McKinsey and Company .2. Business consultants. 3. Industrial management
I. Friga, Paul N. II. Title
HD69.C6 R376 2001
658.4—dc21 2001040326

ISBN-13: 978-0-07-058395-5
ISBN-10: 0-07-058395-1

24 25 26 27 28 ADA 22 21 20 19 18

Published by McGraw Hill Education (India) Private Limited, 444/1, Sri Ekambara Naicker Industrial Estate, Alapakkam, Porur, Chennai 600 116, Tamil Nadu, India, and Printed and bound in India at Adarsh Printers, New Delhi 110 032

Visit us at: www.mheducation.co.in; Phone (Toll free in India): **1800 103 5875**
Write to us at: info.india@mheducation.com

CIN: U22200TN1970PTC111531

For Emma, Jessica, and Talia—EMR

For Meredith (motivation), Mom (direction), Dad (curiosity), and Lido (energy)—PNF

CONTENTS

ACKNOWLEDGMENTS

First and foremost, I would like to thank my coauthor, Paul Friga. This book discusses the virtues of teamwork at length, and I can think of no better example of successful teamwork than our collaboration. This book is much stronger for it. He has pushed my thinking in new and productive directions; I trust he can say the same of me. —*Ethan M. Rasiel*

→ → →

Without question, the first acknowledgment goes to my coauthor, Ethan Rasiel. First, he graciously brought me into the process after already achieving great success with his solo effort on his first book, *The McKinsey Way*. Second, he offered incredible insight, enthusiasm, and direction. And third, he taught me lessons in persistence, storytelling, and unselfishness. —*Paul N. Friga*

→ → →

The authors owe thanks to many without whom this book would not be in your hands. First, their agent, Daniel Greenberg at James Levine Communications, Inc.; their editor, Mary Glenn; Katherine Hinkebein; and the entire team at McGraw-Hill who made this book a reality. Joe Burton, Simon Carne, Jerry Friga, Ed

Pringle, and Paul Sansone made insightful suggestions in the early stages of this manuscript. Our research assistants, Lindsay Cage, Rebecca Jones, and especially Karen Jansen, rendered invaluable support administering questionnaires, researching ideas, and organizing material. David Ernsthausen at the Kenan-Flagler School of Business at the University of North Carolina provided expert assistance with the knowledge management section of this book, and Peggy Pickard, also of UNC, ensured that we had the facilities we needed for our frequent conferences and brainstorming sessions.

Most of all, we are grateful to all those McKinsey alumni who gave us interviews or answered our questionnaires: Jim Bennett, Omowale Crenshaw, Dean Dorman, Naras Eechambadi, Bob Garda, Evan Grossman, Eric Hartz, Paul Kenny, Stevie McNeal, Sylvia Mathews, Bill Ross, Larry Rouvelas, Jeff Sakaguchi, Dan Veto, Steve Anderson, Alan Barasky, Martha Blue, Roger Boisvert, Francesca Brockett, Bob Buchsbaum, Ciara Burnham, S. Neil Crocker, Dominik Falkowski, Brad Farnsworth, Shyam Giridharadas, Barbara Goose, Francesco Grillo, Reggie Groves, Fred Kindle, Deborah Knuckey, Heiner Kopperman, Kurt Lieberman, Lee Newman, Leah Niederstadt, Ron O'Hanley, Rainer Siggelkow, Chacko Sonny, and Jim Whelan, as well as many others, who, for reasons of their own, wish to remain anonymous. We could not have written this book without them.

INTRODUCTION

ABOUT THIS BOOK

February 1999 saw the publication of *The McKinsey Way* by Ethan M. Rasiel, a former associate of management-consulting powerhouse McKinsey & Company. That book combined the—occasionally humorous—anecdotes of McKinsey alumni with the personal recollections of the author to describe the techniques that McKinsey consultants use to help their clients become more efficient and effective. *The McKinsey Way* also painted a vivid picture of life behind the walls of the publicity-shy organization that its employees refer to as "the Firm."

The McKinsey Mind picks up where *The McKinsey Way* left off. Most of that book was taken up with a description of consulting McKinsey-style in the context of a typical project—"engagement" in Firm jargon. It started with the sale of the engagement and moved step by step through the implementation of McKinsey's solution. It also briefly discussed the thought process that McKinsey consultants use to tackle tough business problems.

By necessity, *The McKinsey Way* was more descriptive than prescriptive. With *The McKinsey Mind*, we take the opposite tack. Whereas *The McKinsey Way* dealt with *what* McKinsey does, *The McKinsey Mind* shows you *how* to apply McKinsey techniques in your career and organization. To accomplish this, we build on the knowledge base of *The McKinsey Way* but offer a different perspective, as we shall explain later in this Introduction. At this point, however, we want to assure you that if you haven't read *The McKinsey Way*, you need not read it in order to understand or profit from *The McKinsey Mind.** In fact, we even provide summaries of the relevant lessons from *The McKinsey Way* at the start of each section of this book, as well as a list of where to find them in Appendix B.

Anyone can use the problem-solving and management techniques described in *The McKinsey Way* (and *The McKinsey Mind*); you don't have to be in (or even from) the Firm. We also recognize that McKinsey is a unique organization. Its consultants can call on resources not usually available to executives in other companies. Its flat hierarchy allows junior consultants to make decisions and express their ideas in ways that would be impossible in more-stratified workplaces. And when working with clients, the Firm's consultants generally have a freedom of access and action unavailable to most executives. With these thoughts in mind, we realized that to take *The McKinsey Way* to the next level, we had to adapt it to organizations that don't enjoy McKinsey's peculiar advantages.

Fortunately, we did not have to look far for inspiration in this regard. In researching this book, we relied on interviews with and questionnaires from more than 75 McKinsey alumni who have

---

*One of your authors, specifically Ethan Rasiel, would be very happy if, having read this book, you decided to buy the *The McKinsey Way* as well.

successfully implemented the Firm's techniques and strategies in their post-McKinsey organizations. Since leaving the Firm, they have become CEOs, entrepreneurs, and senior decision makers in businesses and governments around the world. If anyone could show us what works outside McKinsey and what doesn't, they could—and did.

In this book, therefore, you will discover a problem-solving and decision-making process based on McKinsey's own, highly successful methods but adapted to the "real world" based on—and, we believe, strengthened by—the experiences of McKinsey alumni in their post-McKinsey careers. You will also learn the management techniques you will need to implement that process in your own career and the presentation strategies that will allow you to communicate your ideas throughout your organization.

ABOUT McKINSEY

In case you are unfamiliar with McKinsey & Company, let us offer a few words about the organization that its members past and present refer to as "the Firm." Since its founding in 1923, McKinsey & Company has become the world's most successful strategic consulting firm. It currently has 84 offices (and counting) around the world and employs some 7,000 professionals who hail from 89 countries. It may not be the largest strategy firm in the world—some of the big accounting firms have larger practices—but it is certainly the most prestigious. McKinsey consults to more than a thousand clients, including 100 of the world's 150 largest companies, as well as many state and federal agencies of the United States and foreign governments. McKinsey is a brand name in international business circles.

Several senior McKinsey partners have risen to international prominence in their own right. Lowell Bryan advised the Senate Banking Committee during the savings and loan crisis. Jon Katzenbach's books on the management of high-performance teams appear on the bookshelves of CEOs around the world. Even more visible are some of McKinsey's alumni who have gone on to senior positions around the world: Tom Peters, management guru and coauthor of *In Search of Excellence*; Lou Gerstner, CEO of IBM; and Jeff Skilling, CEO of Enron, to name but three.

To maintain its preeminent position (and to earn its high fees), the Firm seeks out the cream of each year's crop of business school graduates. It lures them with high salaries, the prospect of a rapid rise through McKinsey's meritocratic hierarchy, and the chance to mingle with the elite of the business world. In return, the Firm demands total devotion to client service, submission to a grueling schedule that can include weeks or months away from home and family, and only the highest-quality work. For those who meet McKinsey's standards, promotion can be rapid. Those who fall short soon find themselves at the latter end of the Firm's strict policy of "up or out."

Like any strong organization, the Firm has a powerful corporate culture based on shared values and common experiences. Every "McKinsey-ite" goes through the same rigorous training programs and suffers through the same long nights in the office. To outsiders, this can make the Firm seem monolithic and forbidding. One recent book on management consulting likened McKinsey to the Jesuits.

The Firm has its own jargon, too. It is full of acronyms: EM, ED, DCS, ITP, ELT, BPR, etc. McKinsey-ites call their assignments or projects "engagements." On an engagement, a McKinsey team will search for the "key drivers" in their quest to "add value." Like most jargon, much of this is simply verbal shorthand; some of it, however, once understood, can be as useful to businesspeople outside the Firm as it is to McKinsey-ites themselves.

ABOUT THE PROBLEM-SOLVING PROCESS

Our benchmark is the problem-solving process as practiced by McKinsey. At the most abstract level, McKinsey develops solutions to clients' strategic problems and, possibly, aids in the implementation of those solutions. Figure I-1 depicts our theoretical model of problem solving, which breaks the process into six discrete elements. In The McKinsey Mind, we will focus on the central triangle of this model (the items in bold).

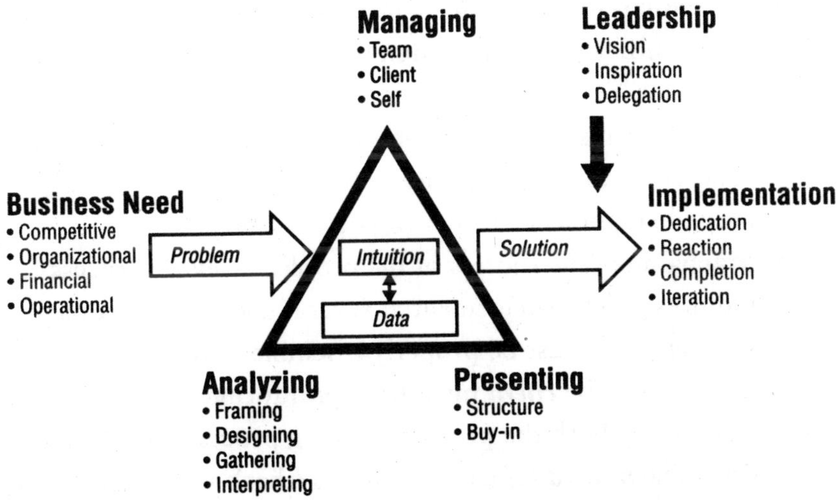

Figure I-1. Strategic Problem-Solving Model

- **Business Need**—You can't have problem solving without a problem or, more broadly, a need on the part of the client. In business, those needs come in several forms: competitive, organizational, financial, and operational.
- **Analyzing**—Once your organization has identified the problem, it can begin to seek a solution, whether on its own or with the help of McKinsey (or any other outside agent). McKinsey's fact-based, hypothesis-driven problem-solving process begins with *framing the problem*: defining the boundaries of the problem and breaking it down into its component elements to allow the problem-solving team to come up with an initial hypothesis as to the solution. The next step is *designing the analysis*, determining the analyses that must be done to prove the hypothesis, followed by *gathering the data* needed for the analyses. Finally comes *interpreting the results* of those analyses to see whether they prove or disprove the hypothesis and to develop a course of action for the client.
- **Presenting**—You may have found a solution, but it has no value until it has been communicated to and accepted by the client. For that to happen, you must *structure* your presentation so that it communicates your ideas clearly and concisely and generates *buy-in* for your solution for each individual audience to which you present.
- **Managing**—The success of the problem-solving process requires good management at several levels. The problem-solving *team* must be properly assembled, motivated, and developed. The *client* must be kept informed, involved, and inspired by both the problem-solving process and the solution. The *individual* team members (that's you) must strike a balance between life and career that allows them to meet

the expectations of the client and the team while not "burning out."

- **Implementation**—Your organization may have accepted your solution, but it must still implement it. This requires the *dedication* of sufficient resources within the organization, the timely *reaction* of the organization to any stumbling blocks that may arise during implementation, the focus of the organization on *completion* of the tasks necessary for full implementation. In addition, the organization must institute a process of *iteration* that leads to continual improvement. That process requires reassessing implementation and rededicating the organization to make additional changes identified during reassessment.
- **Leadership**—At the nexus of solution and implementation comes leadership. Those at the helm of your organization must conceive a strategic *vision* for the organization. They must also provide *inspiration* for those in the organization who will do the hands-on work of implementation. Finally, they must make the right judgments regarding *delegation* of authority in overseeing implementation throughout the organization.

There is one other piece of the model: the tension between *intuition* and *data*. Problem solving doesn't take place in a vacuum. Even McKinsey has only so many resources to throw at a problem and a limited time in which to solve it. While we are advocates for McKinsey-style fact-based problem solving, we recognize that it's practically impossible to have *all* the relevant facts before reaching a decision. Therefore, most executives make business decisions based partly on facts and partly on intuition—gut instinct tempered by experience. We will discuss the pros and cons of each element later in the book. For now, we will simply say that we think a sound decision requires a balance of both.

As we mentioned, *The McKinsey Mind* will focus on the central triangle of the consulting process—problem solving, presenting, and managing—that constitutes the day-to-day work of a McKinsey consulting team. In Chapters 1 through 4, we discuss McKinsey's fact-based, hypothesis-driven problem-solving process and show how you can use it to tackle the complex problems that arise in your own organization. In Chapter 5, we introduce strategies for presentation that will allow you to get your ideas across with maximum impact, whether your audience is your boss, your board, or your entire company. Finally, in Chapters 6 through 8, we cover the management techniques you need to ensure that your own problem-solving efforts run smoothly. Client needs, leadership, and implementation are beyond the scope of *The McKinsey Mind*; they are topics for another day and, perhaps, another book.

The chapters of *The McKinsey Mind* follow the same general structure. Each chapter (except Chapter 2) is divided into two or more sections. Each section begins with a brief discussion of the topic at hand, followed by a summary of the relevant lessons from *The McKinsey Way*. Next comes a discussion of the new lessons we learned from our alumni along with illustrations of successful implementation, followed by suggestions for implementing these lessons in your own organization. Each section ends with exercises to help you understand and practice the lessons of the section.

Since the book follows the problem-solving process from start to finish, we recommend that you read the book that way, too, at least for the first time through. Having said that, each chapter of *The McKinsey Mind* is more or less self-contained, and you can easily treat the book as a reference on the topics that are most interesting and relevant for you. If you lack the time or patience to read the book from cover to cover, then we suggest at least reading Chapter 1 before diving into the rest of the book, as the other chapters refer frequently to the concepts therein. However you decide to read it, we hope *The McKinsey Mind* helps you become a better problem solver and decision maker.

A FEW TERMS

Throughout *The McKinsey Mind*, we use a number of terms that are not necessarily self-evident. To avoid confusion, we'd like briefly to discuss the most significant ones here:

- *Client*—In the context of McKinsey-style consulting, the meaning of *client* is obvious: it's the organization for which you are solving a problem. For the purposes of this book, we have broadened the term to include anyone for whom you are solving a problem, whether you are an insider or an outsider. Thus, if you work in a large company, your company or business unit is your client; if you are an entrepreneur, you and your customers are your clients.
- *McKinsey-ites*—We are not aware of any accepted term for employees of McKinsey. *The McKinsey Way* uses "McKinsey-ite" in preference to other terms (some of them not necessarily complimentary), and we're sticking with it.
- *Alumni*—McKinsey uses this term to describe its former employees (who now number more than 10,000 souls), regardless of the circumstances of their departure. It's much neater than the alternatives ("former McKinsey-ite" or "ex-McKinsey-ite"), so we're using it, too.
- *The Firm*—McKinsey-ites refer to their employer simply as "the Firm," in much the same way as employees of a cer-

tain secretive, publicity-shy U.S. government department refer to theirs as "the Company." McKinsey alumni still use the term when discussing their former employer. Since we're McKinsey alumni ourselves, we do so as well.

ABOUT CONFIDENTIALITY

Confidentiality is one of the cardinal virtues within McKinsey. The Firm guards its secrets closely. We, along with all other McKinsey alumni, agreed never to disclose confidential information about the Firm or its clients, even after leaving McKinsey. We do not intend to break that agreement. Furthermore, in researching this book and in talking and corresponding with dozens of McKinsey alumni, it was inevitable that some would tell us things that they did not want traced back to the source. As a result, many of the names of companies and people in this book have been disguised.

→ → →

We believe that what follows is powerful methodology for solving problems and communicating ideas that will benefit you and your organization. We hope that by the end of this book you will share this belief. Now it is time to enter the McKinsey Mind.

1

FRAMING THE PROBLEM

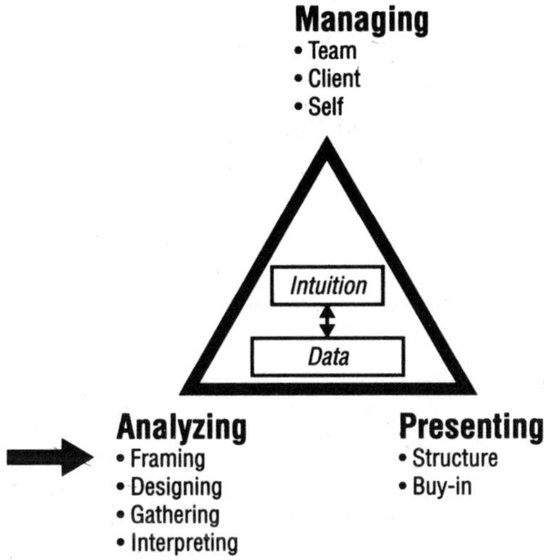

The ability to frame business problems to make them susceptible to rigorous fact-based analysis is one of the core skills of a McKinsey consultant. More than that, it is the hallmark of a McKinsey-ite: if you can't solve problems in a structured, hypothesis-driven manner, you're unlikely to make it through the door of the Firm.

The McKinsey problem-solving process begins with the use of structured frameworks to generate fact-based hypotheses followed by data gathering and analysis to prove or disprove the hypothesis. A hypothesis greatly speeds up your quest for a solution by sketching out a road map for research and analyses that will guide your work throughout the problem-solving process, all the way to the presentation of your solution. Given the value of this methodology to Firm alumni in their post-McKinsey careers, we begin with an examination of ways to adapt that process to businesses beyond the Firm.

In this chapter, we will show you how to apply structure to your business problems and how to go about devising initial hypotheses that will speed up your own decision making. Because structure is the basis for the McKinsey problem-solving process, let's start there.

STRUCTURE

Although McKinsey & Company often uses the term *fact-based* to describe it, the McKinsey problem-solving process begins not with facts but with structure. Structure can refer to particular problem-solving frameworks or more generally to defining the boundaries of a problem and then breaking it down into its component elements. With either approach, structure allows McKinsey consultants to come rapidly to grips with the issues facing them and enables them to form initial hypotheses about possible solutions. The benefits of structure transfer readily beyond the confines of the Firm, as our alumni have shown. The facts, as we will see, come later.

THE McKINSEY WAY

Let's start by summarizing the ways McKinsey consultants apply structure to their business problems.

Feel free to be MECE. Structure is vital to McKinsey's fact-based problem-solving process. For McKinsey-ites, structure is less a tool and more a way of life. One Firm alumnus summed up his McKinsey experience as "Structure, structure, structure. MECE, MECE, MECE." The concept of MECE (pronounced "mee-see" and an acronym for Mutually Exclusive, Collectively Exhaustive), is a basic tenet of the McKinsey thought process. Being MECE in the context of problem solving means separating your problem into distinct, nonoverlapping issues while making sure that no issues relevant to your problem have been overlooked.

Don't reinvent the wheel. McKinsey has leveraged its experience with structured problem solving through numerous frameworks that help its consultants rapidly visualize the outlines of many common business situations. Your organization may have its own frameworks, and you should take advantage of them if possible. Otherwise, develop your own problem-solving tool kit based on your experience.

Every client is unique. Frameworks are not magic bullets. McKinsey-ites know that every client is unique. Simply trying to squeeze every organization's problems through the appropriate frameworks will only get you so far. If anything, this lesson is doubly true for McKinsey-ites once they leave the Firm.

LESSONS LEARNED AND IMPLEMENTATION ILLUSTRATIONS

How does McKinsey's structured problem-solving approach fare beyond the specific conditions of the Firm? Extremely well. Our discussions with McKinsey alumni have led us to several specific conclusions about the suitability and adaptability of structured thinking:

- Without structure, your ideas won't stand up.
- Use structure to strengthen your thinking.

Let's see what these lessons look like in practice.

Without structure, your ideas won't stand up. Think about your company and the way you and your colleagues formulate and present business ideas. Do you use a consistent structure or at least emphasize the need for internal coherence and logic in your problem solving? Or do people usually arrive at decisions ad hoc, without a recognizable structure or factual support? When McKinsey-ites exit the Firm, they are often shocked by the sloppy thinking processes prevalent in many organizations.

Most of us are not blessed from birth with the ability to think in a rigorous, structured manner; we have to learn how. Unfortunately, that skill is not part of most university curricula, and few companies have the resources or the inclination to teach it to their employees. McKinsey and some other strategy-consulting firms are exceptions to this pattern. Even some of the most highly regarded companies in American business don't always stress structured problem solving, as Bill Ross learned when he joined the Transportation Division of General Electric:

> GE people move quickly when new situations arise. It's part of the culture. The mind-set seems to be "once we have identified an issue, let's wrestle it to the ground and move quickly," and they're great at doing it. Rarely do people take the time to examine the issue and develop a clear plan of action. The structured approach really surprises a lot of peo-

ple. I think just focusing people on that has allowed me to add value.

Many highly successful organizations don't apply structured thought even to their core competencies, as Paul Kenny describes at GlaxoSmithKline:

> From a scientific point of view, a lot of the research organization is rather serendipity led: you invest in research, you may have a direction, but often that direction will change as a result of information you find. Some of the best drugs on the market today were found more by luck than by design. Then, thinking back, we realize that we could have redesigned these clinical trials in a way to shape the product more appropriately for the market. There are concrete examples of ways to increase value by making more-commercial marketing decisions earlier on in the pipeline, and designing products from the very beginning to have the right characteristics, rather than just letting them evolve from the R&D pipeline however they emerge.

If structured thinking is hard to find at GE and GlaxoSmithKline, two of the world's most respected and successful companies, one can imagine that it may be a pretty rare coin in many organizations.

Further complicating matters, the corporate cultures of some organizations have been imbued with the wrong types of structure. In another example from GlaxoSmithKline, a linear, deductive thought process got in the way of sound decision making:

> We have a project leader who wants to switch his drug from its current twice-a-day formulation to a once-a-day formulation. The drug is at an early stage in research, and it's a

> standard rule that once a day is better than twice a day. It's easier for people to take, so ultimately there's a market-driven push to develop the once-a-day dosage. He has presented this as a binary decision: either we invest in it, or we don't. But the idea of thinking through the various options that might really be possible in a MECE way, opening out all the possibilities and then considering or rejecting them independently, hasn't really occurred to him.
>
> In fact, there are a number of options, including launching as a twice-a-day formulation, getting through a lot of the development risk that way, then moving to a once-a-day formulation once the drug has proved efficacious and marketable. Taking the all-or-nothing approach may not necessarily be the best way to create value; the incremental sales may not be worth the incremental costs and risks.

Between inappropriate thinking processes and the complete absence of structured thought, there appears to be a lot of room for someone with a McKinsey Mind to add value.

Use structure to strengthen your thinking. In all sorts of places—whether huge corporations, new economy start-ups, or even nonbusiness organizations such as nonprofits and government agencies—McKinsey-ites have been able to apply structured thinking in ways that allow them to add value to their organizations. For example, making strategic decisions requires understanding the capabilities of your organization and how to utilize those capabilities to maximize performance. That's what Jim Bennett did during his tenure as chairman of retail banking at Key Corp.:

> I became chair of the retail bank at a time when we really needed to grow our operation. It was a third of the company, and we had to grow at 10 percent per year for the rest of the company to do well. I had to determine whether that was

> possible or not. Of course, this depended on understanding how good we were. The only way I could come to grips with that was to lay out an issue tree.* By the time I was done, I had a MECE issue tree with all the branches covered by yes/no questions. That proved very useful to me as the line manager and chief strategist of Key Corp.'s largest business in making sure that we were on the right track with our performance improvement program.
>
> I did it myself and then exposed others to it and the general idea behind it. The issue tree in and of itself probably strikes people as a bit "consultanty," but when I've been able to translate it into a communicable message, it's never failed me in any setting, anywhere.

Another example of the successful application of McKinsey frameworks in a large organization comes from Bill Ross, who was then at GE:

> The biggest "framing the problem" issue I found involved the big question, "Do we know where we are going in the long term and have we developed our growth strategy?" The answer in many cases was no. I worked individually with some of the other general managers and then actually used McKinsey to put together a workshop with the senior leadership team to talk explicitly about our growth strategy. This allowed me to start feeding them information and expose them to some of the previous frameworks that I learned at McKinsey. When they saw those, it triggered light bulbs in their heads.

Large, cash-rich corporations might seem the ideal place to apply McKinsey techniques. After all, most of McKinsey's clients fit that description. What might surprise you, however, is how

---

* We will discuss issue trees later in this chapter.

effective these same techniques can be in the short-of-cash, short-of-time, short-of-people environment of a New Economy start-up, as Omowale Crenshaw discovered at Africa.com, a Web portal for the African continent:

> We had to survey the marketplace and decide how to develop products and services for our particular target markets: African ex-pats and the "Africa-interested." That meant analyzing a number of industries such as African wine, or African home-decorative accessories, furniture, and art, and making a decision as to which of them would be sufficiently attractive to our target markets. By allowing us to come to grips quickly with the market sizes, the competitive environment, the key players, etc., the structural frameworks that I learned at the Firm helped us decide which of these markets made sense for us.

Structuring your thinking can add value outside the confines of the business world. Sylvia Mathews was deputy chief of staff to President Clinton, so she should know:

> Problem solving at the federal government level tends to be a little more complicated than in the business world, in that it involves things that are less tangible than valuation of companies, profit, loss, etc. But the same techniques still apply. When I was in charge of the State of the Union production in 1996, in August (the President delivers the State of the Union address in January), I started by doing something that I called the Pillars Project. It covered every area of the State of the Union and put all our policy examples together in the same framework and with the same approach to show what we were going to try to achieve over the second four years. We then assembled them into documents that the President and Vice President could respond to over their vacations.

> We framed the issue very clearly: What is the problem? What are its dimensions? What are we going to do? And it laid out a number of things that we could try in a limited way to increase our chances of success. We covered the various issues stemming from each problem: you might want to do something, but is it achievable, do we have the resources financially, can we get the congressional support, and what are the political ramifications?

Now that you've seen how useful structured thinking can be in almost any sort of organization, let's discuss how you can apply it in your own business and career.

IMPLEMENTATION GUIDANCE

As we've seen, structured thinking is an important element in any businessperson's problem-solving arsenal. How should you use this weapon? First, you must understand that structure doesn't exist in a vacuum; you have to wield it with a goal in mind. In the context of framing and solving business problems, your goal is to bring order out of chaos.

Today's executives and entrepreneurs have access to far more information than they can possibly use. They can manage this surfeit of data only by filtering out all but the most relevant facts. The appropriate structured framework will allow you to do this much more efficiently, thereby increasing the probability that you will arrive at a solution in a reasonable amount of time—and add value to your business. As Omowale Crenshaw observes:

> One of the things that was very clear from my McKinsey experience—and this definitely applies in an entrepreneurial environment—was that the skill set that I have allows me to make some sense of ambiguity, of all the possible paths we

> could take. We have limited resources and limited funds, so we can't go everywhere; we have to start following these paths one at a time. A framework helps you prioritize your options. We save so much time and energy by not going down the wrong path. That's the key. Not necessarily knowing what the right path is, but not going too far down the wrong one.

The role of senior management in this is to structure "reality" in order to make it easily graspable. Executives do this by defining the scope of the problem at hand in order to see all its ramifications—the links to other factors and the whole scope of consequences. They can then disregard unimportant factors and concentrate on prioritizing the options available to the organization. This allows them to communicate the (potentially complex) problem and its solution in easily understandable terms, to make it clear to those who need to execute management's directives.

We will examine gathering the data and communicating the solution in later chapters, so let's turn now to defining and simplifying the problem. In the generic approach to framing the problem, McKinsey-ites put this concept into practice by breaking the problem before them into its component elements. Why? In most cases, a complex problem can be reduced to a group of smaller, simpler problems that can be solved individually. The problems McKinsey handles are either extremely complex ("How can we maintain shareholder value in the face of competitive pressure and union demands when our core market is shrinking?") or stated so broadly as to be insoluble without further clarification ("How do we make money in our industry?"). Separating out the individual pieces of the problem will make it easier for you and your team to identify the key drivers of the problem (see Chapter 2) and focus your analysis accordingly.

This technique works not only for business problems, but also for complex problems in other realms, such as politics. For instance, Francesco Grillo, formerly with McKinsey's Rome office, is now a public-sector consultant and policy adviser to the Italian government. He used these same techniques with great success on problems such as unemployment in the European Union, reform of the Italian electoral system, and the evaluation of the economic impact of programs funded by the European Commission.

The most common tool McKinsey-ites use to break problems apart is the *logic tree*, a hierarchical listing of all the components of a problem, starting at the "20,000-foot view" and moving progressively downward. As an illustration, let's look at that fine old blue-chip firm Acme Widgets. Let's suppose that Acme's board has called your team in to help answer the basic question "How can we increase our profits?" The first question that might pop into your head upon hearing this is, "Where do your profits come from?" The board answers, "From our three core business units: widgets, grommets, and thrum-mats."

"Aha!" you think to yourself, "that is the first level of our logic tree for this problem." You could then proceed down another level by breaking apart the income streams of each business unit, most basically into "Revenues" and "Expenses," and then into progressively smaller components as you move further down the tree. By the time you've finished, you should have a detailed, MECE map of Acme Widgets' business system, along the lines of Figure 1-1 (page 12).

Remember, when you are drawing a logic tree, there may be several ways to break apart a problem. Which one you choose will affect the way you view the problem and can either reveal or obscure critical issues for your team. For instance, instead of drawing your logic tree of Acme Widgets with an organizational hierarchy (by business unit), you might want to look at it from a functional perspective (production, sales, marketing, research, ful-

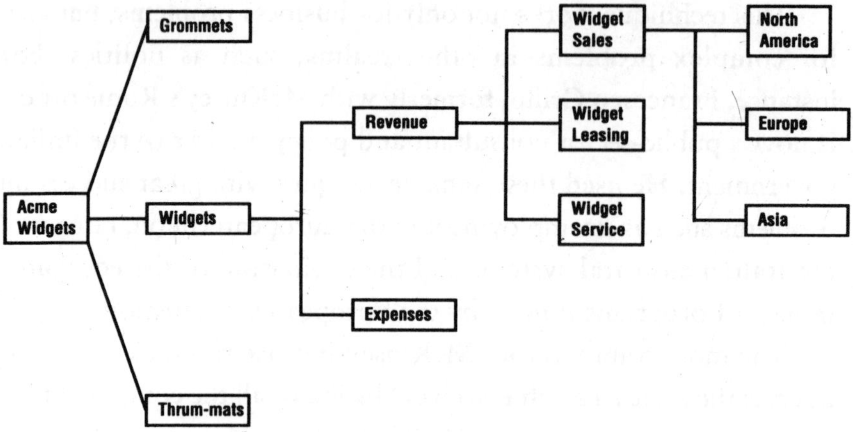

Figure 1-1. Acme Widgets Logic Tree

fillment, etc.). This perspective could point your team in other, potentially useful directions. Just make sure, whichever view you take, that your logic tree is MECE, so that you miss nothing and avoid confusion.

In a real-life example of a logic tree at work, Naras Eechambadi, when he went to First Union after leaving McKinsey, had to put together the business case for his customer information management unit in order to get funding approved by the president of the corporation:

> The question boiled down to, "If we are going to produce a return on investment for the company based on how we build and leverage customer information, where are the sources of revenue and profit? Where is the money going to come from?" I came up with a MECE breakdown showing how we could make money by adding or selling more products and generating more revenue from existing customers, cutting costs to serve the existing customers, reducing the attrition of existing customers, or being much more effective and efficient in bringing on new customers. And I was

> able to bounce around the problem and say for each of the pieces, "How much more money can be expected? What is the economic benefit? And at the end of the day, what is the cost of doing all these things?" That's how I built my business case, by breaking down and reconstructing the problem, figuring out where the pieces were.

The logic tree is one framework among many that McKinsey consultants use and an especially popular one for them to take with them when they leave the Firm. Like any framework, it helps you clear away the clutter of a complex problem and bring order out of chaos by building a simplified representation of the real world. Jeff Sakaguchi, who left McKinsey's Los Angeles office to become a partner at Accenture, sums up the usefulness of the frameworks he learned at the Firm:

> The whole framework-driven approach is really trying to think about, "How could you organize this?" Every framework—all the way down to the simple two-by-two matrices we use day in, day out—are an attempt to frame the problem around some nifty set of three, four, or five balls or boxes or triangles or whatever you need to create a simple representation of a complex problem. McKinsey was masterful at that. I've really tried to adapt that for my work.

When employing logic trees or any framework, bear in mind your eventual audience. Tailor your presentation of that framework accordingly. As Bill Ross discovered at GE:

> I find that, although frameworks work great internally at McKinsey, when you go outside McKinsey you have to be careful about their use. Many people will see a framework and automatically start getting defensive. We heard it a lot at McKinsey: "Oh, you're taking an approach that you used on

somebody else's problems and trying to apply it to me. My problems are different." We knew that wasn't the case; we were just trying to get the thoughts started, giving ourselves a systematic checklist for what the key issues are and how to present those key issues. You have to be careful about introducing frameworks because they can carry a fairly negative connotation, especially if they are overused. Instead of reusing an old framework, use the concepts from the framework to generate new ideas that help solve the problem at hand.

Finally, remember that structure is only the beginning. You still need to develop a strong hypothesis, devise and perform the right analyses to draw your conclusions, and communicate those conclusions effectively. We will address these issues further on in the book, beginning in the next section of this chapter, with formulating the initial hypothesis.

EXERCISES

- If you can, think of some frameworks that are commonly used in your business or that you learned elsewhere. Can you apply them to your current work? If not, how could you apply them?
- Look at your organization. Can you lay out your sources of profit in a MECE logic tree? How about the process by which you generate products or deliver services?
- Think of a common, but complex, *nonbusiness* process, say, a wedding or a vacation. Can you come up with a MECE structuring of all the tasks that need to be done in order for this process to work? What are the key elements of the process (e.g., for a wedding, getting the guests there

on time, making sure the groom shows up)? Write them out in the form of a logic tree. Can you come up with a different grouping—say, by responsibility—that is still MECE?

HYPOTHESIS

Having reduced the problem to its essential components through the use of appropriate frameworks, you are ready to embark on the next step in the process of framing it: forming a hypothesis as to its likely solution. McKinsey believes, and the experiences of McKinsey alumni demonstrate, that using an initial hypothesis to guide your research and analysis will increase both the efficiency and effectiveness of your decision making.

THE McKINSEY WAY

As we did with structure, let's begin our exploration of using hypotheses by recapping the relevant principles espoused by McKinsey.

Solve the problem at the first meeting. McKinsey-ites learn that it is much more efficient to analyze the facts of a problem with the intent of proving or disproving a hypothesis than to analyze those facts one by one to determine which answer they will eventually provide. For a start, a hypothesis provides you and your team with a problem-solving road map that will lead you to ask the right questions and perform the correct analyses to get to your answer. A good hypothesis will also save you time by pointing out potential blind alleys much more quickly and allowing you to get back to the main issues if you do go down the wrong path.

You generate your initial hypothesis by drawing conclusions based on the limited facts that you know about the problem at hand without doing a lot of additional research. For a consultant new to the industry in question, this might mean spending a few hours reading press articles and annual reports; someone with plentiful industry experience might just jot down a few preliminary thoughts. Ideally, you would then spend an hour or two meeting with your teammates and hashing out some likely answers to the problem.

Your next step is to figure out which analyses you have to perform and which questions you have to ask in order to prove or disprove your hypothesis. One way to lay out these questions is with an issue tree. The *issue tree*, a species of logic tree in which each branch of the tree is an issue or question, bridges the gap between structure and hypothesis.* Every issue generated by a framework will likely be reducible to subissues, and these in turn may break down further. An issue tree is simply the laying out of issues and subissues into a MECE visual progression. By answering the questions in the issue tree, you can very quickly determine the validity of your hypothesis.

Proper prior preparation. McKinsey teams rely on brainstorming to develop and test their initial hypotheses. Brainstorming McKinsey-style, however, requires that all the team members come to the meeting prepared, having absorbed all the facts currently known to the team and having spent some time thinking about their implications. Sometimes, especially for team leaders, it helps if individuals have their own initial hypotheses already developed, so that the team can bat them around, but it's not essential. Just don't come into the meeting thinking you know the "answer." Be prepared to learn.

---

*We will detail the distinctions between the logic tree and the issue tree later in this chapter.

In a white room. Brainstorming is about generating new ideas. Check your preconceptions at the door. Everyone in the meeting must be able to speak his mind and share his knowledge. For your brainstorming sessions to succeed, you should follow these rules: First, there are no bad ideas. Second, there are no dumb questions. Third, be prepared to "kill your babies" (i.e., to see your ideas get shot down, and to pull the trigger yourself if necessary). Fourth, know when to say when; don't let brainstorming drag on past the point of diminishing returns. Last and most important, get it down on paper.

The problem is not always the problem. Every consultant faces the temptation of taking the client's diagnosis of his problem at face value. Resist this temptation. Just as a patient is not always aware of the meaning of his symptoms, so are managers sometimes incorrect in their diagnoses of what ails their organizations.

The only way to determine whether the problem you have been given is the real problem is to dig deeper, ask questions, and get the facts. A little skepticism early on in the problem-solving process could save you a lot of frustration further down the road. What's more, you will be doing your client a service by getting to the real problem, even if, sometimes, your client doesn't like it.

LESSONS LEARNED AND IMPLEMENTATION ILLUSTRATIONS

For McKinsey alumni, hypothesis-based decision making has proved extremely portable. It doesn't require a lot of resources to implement; it can be done in teams but, if need be, also on one's own; and it is applicable across a wide spectrum of problems. Our questioning of former McKinsey-ites has produced two good reasons why you should rely on an initial hypothesis in your own problem-solving efforts:

- An initial hypothesis will save you time.
- An initial hypothesis will make your decision making more effective.

An initial hypothesis will save you time. Most people, when faced with a complex problem, will start at the beginning and wade through all the data until they come to the end—the solution. This is sometimes referred to as the deductive approach: if *A*, then *B*; if *B*, then *C*; . . . if *Y*, then *Z*. When you form an initial hypothesis, you leap all the way to *Z*, and it's easier to work your way backward from *Z* to *A*. One simple example of this is a pen-and-paper labyrinth or maze, the kind you sometimes see in the Sunday comics or in puzzle books. Anyone who plays with these can tell you that it is easier to solve the maze by tracing the route from the finish to the start rather than starting at the beginning. One reason for this is that by already knowing where your solution is, you eliminate a lot of paths that lead to dead ends.

Forming an initial hypothesis will allow you to work through the labyrinth of your business problem more quickly. It saves you time partly because it allows you to start drawing conclusions based on limited information—which, at the beginning of the problem-solving process, is usually what you have. This holds especially true when you are trying to break new ground where nobody has the information you seek, as Omowale Crenshaw discovered when figuring out how to open up Africa to E-commerce:

> Sometimes at McKinsey we had the luxury of leveraging so much data—the whole analysis paralysis—that we didn't do anything, nor did our clients. When we were starting our Web portal, we had to figure out what mattered when we really didn't have enough data on one side or the other. We just had to say, "OK, realistically, what do we know about the largest three or four or five markets? What are our

> guesstimates about them?" We were figuring it out on the back of an envelope, trying to be mostly right versus precisely wrong, and making some hypotheses from that. We would say, "OK, if we assume that the market size is X, what do we have to believe?"
>
> Then the process became iterative: "We think the market size is *X*, and if the market size is *X*, then *Y* must be true," so we went and looked at Y. As we started doing that, it became much more apparent that we were on the right track. We're still struggling with the actual size of the market, but we feel much more comfortable that we've done the actual due diligence as it relates to tapping into any and every resource we could think of.

Finally, an initial hypothesis saves you time by forcing you and your team to focus only on those issues that can prove or disprove it. This is especially helpful for those who have trouble focusing and prioritizing. You may even know of a few such individuals in your own organization.

An initial hypothesis will make your decision making more effective. Not only does the hypothesis-driven approach make your problem solving faster and more efficient, it allows you to assess multiple options quickly. As a result, your decision making becomes more flexible and therefore more effective. As CEO of a brand-name consumer goods manufacturer, McKinsey alumnus Bob Garda, now a member of the marketing faculty at the Fuqua School of Business at Duke University, used a strong initial hypothesis that went against his company's conventional wisdom to turn around its core business:

> We were selling products that had been around for 20 years and faced a lot of price pressure from Wal-Mart, Kmart, and Target—our three biggest customers. They kept threatening

> to go to suppliers in China or India unless we lowered our prices. We had four alternatives: (1) reduce costs to match China and India, (2) buy from China and India and resell to our customers, (3) introduce new products (one of which was close at hand), or (4) do a combination of the above. My hypothesis was that we could best minimize the price pressure by introducing new products. Sure enough, when we walked into the Big 3 to introduce the new product, they were excited; we could practically charge whatever we wanted. After that, they were much less concerned about beating us up on price, even on the established products, as long as we kept generating new products. Therefore, the hypothesis worked out.

Bob compared his hypothesis against other options available to his company:

> We could have taken one of the other approaches and tried to cut costs to beat India and China. In fact, several of our key managers thought cost reduction was the only answer, as it had been in the past. Well, good luck; you can't beat China and India on costs with U.S.–made products. Naturally, cost reduction was part of the answer for the long term; we launched a cost reduction effort, but we never got down to Chinese or Indian costs.
>
> The other option, purchasing from China and India and reselling to Kmart, Wal-Mart, and Target, while popular with a small faction of management, made no sense to me. All we would be doing was setting up a distribution system for the Asian manufacturers and, once established, they would go directly to the buyers and cut us out. Because of constant price pressure, this option will continue to be on the

> table, but as long as we have other values to offer the Big 3, the better off we are going to be.

The increased effectiveness of hypothesis-based decision making stems from the lesson that "the problem is not always the problem." That's what Dominic Falkowski found out when he moved to Egon Zehnder's Warsaw office:

> My client was looking for a CFO because the current manager was not coping well enough with reporting and investment analysis, and he was having problems with his team. We weren't so sure this was the case. After an analysis of the situation, including an assessment of the CFO, we realized that it was the *CEO* who was not structured, changed opinions and processes too often, and did not communicate changes throughout the organization. The CFO was partly to blame, however, as he had poor interpersonal skills and did not cope well with any form of feedback.
>
> We suggested some internal reengineering to be conducted by a strategic consultancy, and we ourselves coached the CFO and CEO. The result: solved problem, happy client and CFO, and a prospering organization. Further, we proved that an external search would not have brought the value the client wanted.

IMPLEMENTATION GUIDANCE

Forming an initial hypothesis will make your problem solving more efficient and more effective, but to reap these benefits, you need to be able to generate and test robust hypotheses. Since you should form your hypothesis at the start of the problem-solving process, you have to rely less on facts (you won't have done most of your fact gathering yet) and more on instinct or intuition. Take what you know about the problem at hand, combine it with your gut feelings on the issue, and think about what the most likely answers are. This does *not* mean that the most likely answer is necessarily the correct one, but it's a good starting point.

If something leaps out at you immediately, congratulations; you've just formed a hypothesis. At this point, whether you are alone at your desk, standing under the shower (alone or otherwise), or in a brainstorming session with your team, you should do the Quick and Dirty Test (QDT) of your hypothesis. The QDT is simply this: what assumptions are you making that need to be true in order for your hypothesis to be true? If any of these assumptions is false, then the hypothesis is false. Much of the time, you can knock out false hypotheses in just a few minutes with the QDT. This is especially useful when you need to choose from a few options quickly, as Ciara Burnham, now a venture capitalist at Evercore Partners, can attest:

> So much of my job involves triaging potential investment opportunities to figure out which ones are worth spending time on. At the outset of any deal evaluation, I ask, "What do I need to believe in order for this to be a good investment, and what are the ways in which this investment could blow up? Therefore, what analysis do I need to do to support/reject the investment and to dimension the risks?" Sounds like a simple approach, but frankly one that many people trained in the deal execution side of the business don't take.

As an example, let's go back to Acme Widgets. Yesterday, the board told you and your team to figure out a way to lower the marginal cost of Acme's venerable line of thrum-mats. Today, in the first few minutes of your brainstorming session, you've come up with a few options that might make the cut: (1) You might pressure your suppliers to lower your raw-materials costs. (2) You could cut the workforce at your thrum-mat manufacturing facilities while maintaining production levels. (3) You might reduce the time that the thrum-mats spend in the curing process, thereby increasing throughput. Now you are going to put each option to the QDT.

Pressuring your suppliers would be great, but can it be done? What needs to be true for that option to work? Well, you might say, raw materials should be a significant factor in total thrum-mat cost; otherwise, reducing the cost of raw materials wouldn't make much difference in the total marginal cost of a finished thrum-mat. As it happens, one of your team knows that raw thrums make up about 35 percent of the total cost of a thrum-mat, so there should be some mileage there. Next, you would need to have some pricing leverage with your suppliers. Unfortunately, on page A2 of this morning's *Wall Street Journal*, there is a story about the newly announced takeover of General Thrums by Allied Thrums and Bezels. Analysts expect the merger to result in a significant reduction in total thrum production capacity, with corresponding upward pressure on wholesale thrum prices. So much for that idea.

What about reducing manufacturing head count? Labor is a large component of the total cost of thrum-mat production, so that would seem a fruitful area for exploration. The key question then is whether Acme's production facilities are overstaffed. One way to determine this is by learning whether Acme's per-worker productivity is low relative to the industry. You recall seeing the results of a recent benchmarking study on thrum-mat production. That study put Acme significantly ahead of its competitors in per-worker output. Another dead end.

That leaves reducing the time that thrum-mats spend in the curing process. Traditionally, Class A thrum-mats spend at least two weeks in the curing locker—an expensive proposition that not only uses a lot of energy, but also ties up inventory, thereby unnecessarily swelling Acme's balance sheet. A reduction in curing time could thus have a double benefit. Not only would it boost Acme's profit line, it also would reduce work-in-progress inventory. What needs to be true to make this feasible? As a first cut, the question would seem to be whether it is possible to make Grade A thrum-mats without a full two-week cure. Coincidentally, one of your team has just read an article in *Thrum-mat Manufacturing Weekly* on a new curing process that utilizes special temperature, humidity, and atmospheric controls and that produces the same or better results as traditional curing methods.

Excellent! Your team has now found an initial hypothesis that passed the QDT.* Your next step will be to test your hypothesis more thoroughly and, if necessary, refine it. To accomplish these goals, you should now put together an *issue tree*.

An issue tree is the evolved cousin of the logic tree. Where a logic tree is simply a hierarchical grouping of elements, an issue tree is the series of questions or issues that must be addressed to prove or disprove a hypothesis. Issue trees bridge the gap between structure and hypothesis. Every issue generated by a framework will likely be reducible to subissues, and these in turn may break down further. By creating an issue tree, you lay out the issues and subissues in a visual progression. This allows you to determine what questions to ask in order to form your hypothesis and serves as a road map for your analysis. It also allows you very rapidly to eliminate dead ends in your analysis, since the answer to any issue immediately eliminates all the branches falsified by that answer.

*This example is provided for illustrative purposes only. It is not meant as a specific prescription for any company, partnership, sole proprietorship, or any other organization involved in the manufacturing, curing, delivering, or servicing of thrum-mats. If you are actually in the thrum-mat business and are reading this, please do your own research.

Dan Veto found issue trees especially useful when defining a set of initiatives for the E-business arm of Conseco, one of America's largest diversified financial services companies:

> In problem solving, a lot of people try to be uniformly complete. The fact is, you don't always have to be. You want to think of everything as MECE, but you don't need to investigate everything to the same depth. For example, we were thinking about our E-business strategy, as we had just formed a new business unit, eConseco. This would be a stand-alone business with a real P&L, so we had to ask ourselves, "What are the key levers of profitability and growth? Which things matter, and which things don't?"
>
> We were inundated with ideas. Somebody on the revenue side would say, "Well, we could sell books." Being able to figure out quickly that that option is never going to make you any money is critical. Being able to snip from the tree the branches that don't matter so that we're focused on the branches that do matter is just an unbelievable problem-solving and problem-framing skill that is not necessarily intuitive but which can really speed the problem-solving process.

Going back to your team room at Acme Widgets, what would an issue map look like for reducing the thrum-mat curing process? As you and your team discuss it, several questions arise: Will it actually save money? Does it require special skills? Do we have those skills in the organization? Will it reduce the quality of our thrum-mats? Can we implement the change in the first place?

When laying out your issue tree, you need to come up with a MECE grouping of these issues and the others that arise. As a first step, you need to figure out which are the top-line issues, the issues that have to be true for your hypothesis to be true. After a bit of brainstorming, you isolate three questions that address the validity of your hypothesis: Will shortening the curing process reduce our costs? Can we, as an organization, implement the necessary changes? If we implement this change, can we maintain product quality? Put these issues one level below your hypothesis, as shown in Figure 1-2.

Unfortunately, the answer to each of these questions lies in several more questions. You will have to answer those in turn before you can come up with a final yes or no. As you take each question down one or more levels, your analysis road map will begin to take shape. Let's drill down on one of these issues and see where it leads us.

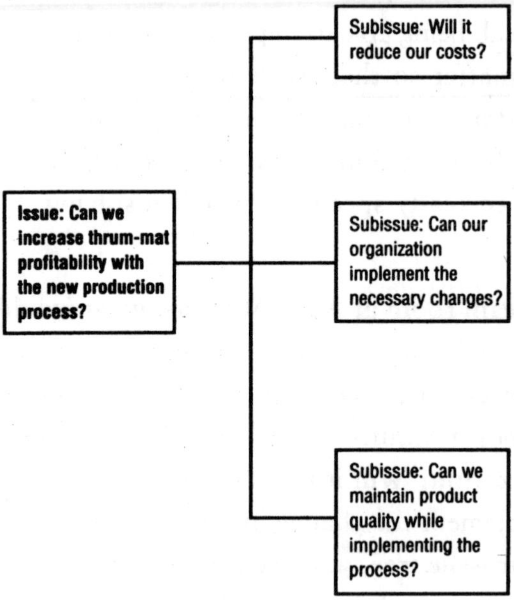

Figure 1-2. Issue Tree for Acme Widgets

The issue "Can we implement the necessary changes?" throws off numerous subsidiary questions (see Figure 1-3). Some of them came out in the initial brainstorming, while others will arise when you spend more time thinking specifically about the issue. Just as you did for the main issue, you need to figure out the logical progression of these questions. For the sake of this exercise, let's say there are two top-line questions for this issue: (1) Does the new, shorter process require special facilities that we don't have? (2) Does it require special skills that we don't have? For both of these questions, the ideal answer, "no," shuts down any further inquiry. If, however, the answer to either of these questions is yes, the hypothesis is not immediately invalidated. Rather, this answer raises additional questions that must be answered. For example, in the case of facilities, you would ask, "Can we build or buy

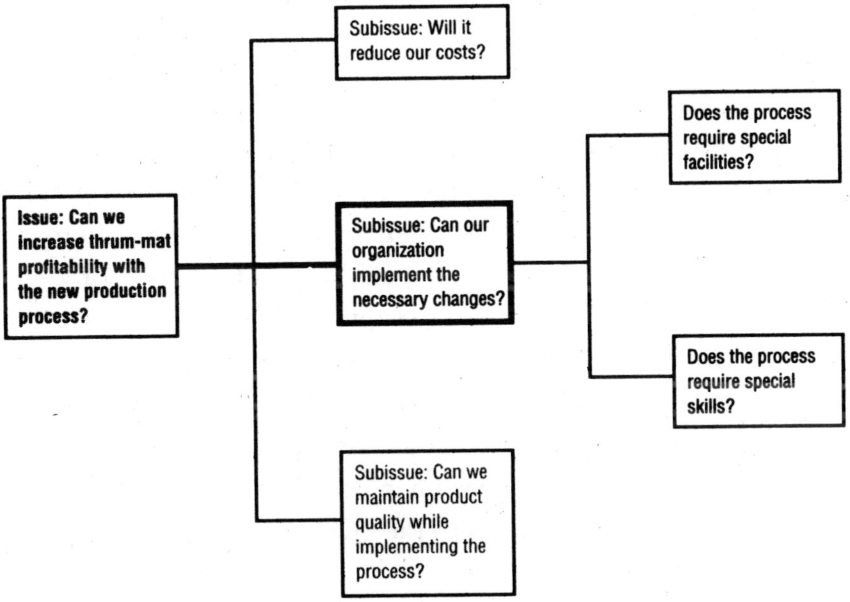

Figure 1-3. Issue Tree for Acme Widgets with Subissues

them?" If the answers to these questions lower down the tree turn out to be no, then your hypothesis is indeed in jeopardy.

At this point, the process of laying out an issue tree should be clear to you. If you've done it, then you have sketched out the tasks that you will need to fulfill in terms of research and analysis—subjects that we will address in the following chapters.

The McKinsey technique of hypothesis-driven problem solving—solving the problem at the first meeting—has proved to be an excellent decision-making skill beyond the confines of the Firm. If you spend some up-front time combining your initial fact base with your gut instinct, you will enable yourself to come to a more robust solution sooner. A little bit of time spent weeding out invalid hypotheses at the outset and then determining the scope of your analysis with an issue tree will save you time and improve your results.

EXERCISES

- Think about a nonbusiness issue about which you hold a strong view (e.g., gun control, evolution, global warming). List the assumptions that you are making with regard to your position. Are they all true? What information or analyses would you need to support your view?
- If you haven't already, come up with a couple of likely hypotheses for whatever issue you are currently working on in your job. Can you come up with one or two things that must be true for each hypothesis to be valid? Now subject each hypothesis to the QDT.

CONCLUSION

By using structured frameworks to create an initial hypothesis, you will enable yourself and your team to select the analyses and areas of research that will allow you to reach a robust conclusion in the shortest possible time. In the next chapter, we will look at how to plan an analysis to prove or disprove your hypothesis in the shortest time possible.

2

DESIGNING THE ANALYSIS

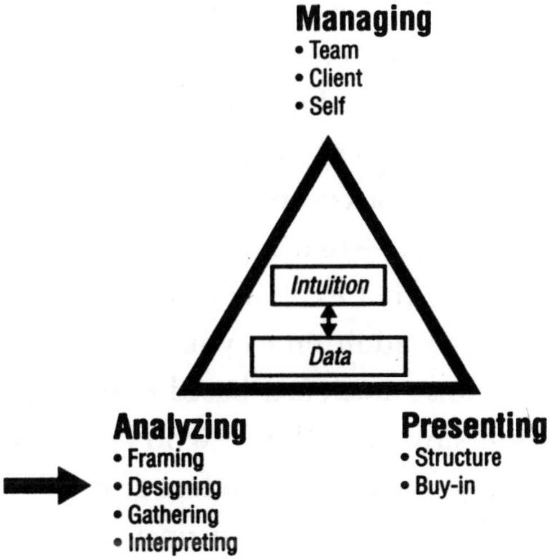

When you form an initial hypothesis, you are "solving the problem at the first meeting." If only it were that easy. Unfortunately, although you may think you have the answer (who knows—you actually might), you have to prove it. You will do so through fact-based analysis.

In their first few years at the Firm, McKinsey-ites focus on analysis as their primary task. In fact, among the criteria the Firm uses in entry-level recruiting, analytical ability stands at or near the top. Even partners and directors are judged on their ability to make value-added recommendations based on the analyses performed by their teams.

There's a saying among small-aircraft pilots, "There are two types of pilots: those who've landed with their landing gear retracted and those who will." The same relationship holds for decision making: sooner or later every executive has to make a major decision based on gut instinct. In many organizations executives make major strategic decisions based as much on gut instinct as on fact-based analysis. Almost all the McKinsey alumni we interviewed found this a radical change from their time at the Firm. Not that this is necessarily bad. In many cases time and resource constraints don't allow for lots of analysis. Many successful managers have developed highly accurate instincts that allow them to reach good decisions quickly—that's why they're successful managers. Still, if you are not that experienced or would just like to have a second opinion (in addition to your gut), we recommend that you avail yourself of as much fact-based analytical support for your decisions as your situation allows. Who knows, sometime it just might remind you to lower your landing gear.

Our discussion of analysis has two distinct parts. In this chapter, we show you how to lay out the analytical tasks that you and your team must perform to prove your initial hypothesis. In Chapter 4, we will show you how to interpret the results of those analyses in ways that maximize their impact on your client or organization. In between, in Chapter 3, we will discuss the fine art of data gathering, since you have to have something to analyze in the first place, before you can get results.

What we call designing the analysis is referred to within McKinsey as "work planning." Work planning is usually the job of the engagement manager (EM) running the day-to-day operation of the team. Early on in the engagement, generally right after the team has taken a stab at an initial hypothesis, the EM will determine what analyses need to be done and who will take responsibility for them. She will discuss with each team member what that person's tasks are, where to look for the data needed to complete them, and how the likely end product should look. Then the team members go off in their separate directions to get the job done.

For most businesses everything needs to be done yesterday if not sooner, and for free. Unfortunately, rigorous, fact-based analysis takes time. As any executive who has hired McKinsey will tell you, that time is expensive. The Firm, however, realizes that its clients can pay just so much, so it has developed many techniques to help a team move quickly from raw facts to value-added recommendations. These techniques work just as well outside McKinsey's walls. We can't promise that you'll be able to work miracles by the time you finish this chapter, but if you apply the lessons we present, you should be able to plot a course that will speed up your analysis and decision making.

THE McKINSEY WAY

The following guidelines help McKinsey-ites plot their analytical courses.

Find the key drivers. The success of most businesses depends on a number of factors, but some are more important than others. When your time and resources are limited, you don't have the luxury of being able to examine every single factor in detail. Instead, when planning your analyses, figure out which factors most affect the problem, and focus on those. Drill down to the core of the problem instead of picking apart each and every piece.

Look at the big picture. When you are trying to solve a difficult, complex problem, you can easily lose sight of your goal amid the million and one demands on your time. When you're feeling swamped by it all, take a metaphorical step back, and figure out what you're trying to achieve. Ask yourself how the task you are doing now fits into the big picture. Is it moving your team toward its goal? If it isn't, it's a waste of time, and time is too precious to waste.

Don't boil the ocean. Work smarter, not harder. In today's data-saturated world, it's easy to analyze every aspect of a problem six ways to Sunday. But it's a waste of time unless the analyses you're doing add significant value to the problem-solving process. Figure out which analyses you need in order to prove (or disprove) your point. Do them, then move on. Chances are you don't have the luxury to do more than just enough.

Sometimes you have to let the solution come to you. Every set of rules has exceptions, and the McKinsey problem-solving process is no different in this regard. Sometimes, for whatever reason, you won't be able to form an initial hypothesis. When that's the case, you have to rely on your analysis of the facts available to point your way to an eventual solution.

LESSONS LEARNED AND IMPLEMENTATION ILLUSTATIONS

In their post-McKinsey careers, most of our alumni have a lot less time to devote to analysis than they did at the Firm. Still, they find that the knowledge they gained about designing analysis plans has helped them get the factual support they need to make decisions in their new organizations. We've distilled their experiences into four lessons that will help you speed up your decision-making cycle:

- Let your hypothesis determine your analysis.
- Get your analytical priorities straight.
- Forget about absolute precision.
- Triangulate around the tough problems.

Let your hypothesis determine your analysis. Once you start to plan your analyses, you have to balance intuition against data. Historically, the McKinsey problem-solving process left no place at all for intuition, although there are indications that, in the New Economy, even McKinsey has come to rely on gut instinct when blazing completely new trails. In contrast, many decision makers prefer to rely almost exclusively on their intuition, especially when time is short. As one McKinsey alumnus noted, "People understand that forming a hypothesis means being results oriented: figure out where you want to go, and determine whether you're on the right track. Often, however, they don't want to take the time to do the little checkoffs to make sure they have the right solution." Although we understand why this is, we believe intuition and data complement each other. You need at least some of each to have a solid basis for your decisions.

The key to striking the balance is quality over quantity. In the words of James G. Whelan at L, G, & E Energy, "Focused analysis is more important than volume, and this stems from good initial problem framing." As we stated in Chapter 1, if you have correctly designed your issue tree, then you should already know what analyses you need to perform. You should have broken down the problem into issues and the issues into subissues. At some point—it may be two levels down the tree or maybe a dozen—the issues will have resolved themselves into a set of questions that can be answered yes or no (e.g., Will the product make money? Do we have the skills to implement the new program? Is it legal?). You will have formed initial hypotheses as to what the answers are; now you must support or refute those hypotheses with fact-based analyses.

Another way to focus your analysis is, as Jeff Sakaguchi at Accenture recommends, starting with the end in mind:

> The process that we go through of issue, subissue, hypothesis, analysis, data collection, end product makes you understand what the end product is likely to look like. It keeps you from doing a bunch of analysis that is interesting, intellectually stimulating, but not very relevant. If you start doing that, you can get beat up in a hurry.

Jeff points out a real danger for those of us who actually enjoy analysis: getting caught up in analysis for its own sake. There's a lot of data out there, and it can be a lot of fun to play around with it in all sorts of new and different ways. Unfortunately, if these analyses aren't working to prove or disprove your hypothesis, then they are just that: playing around.

Get your analytical priorities straight. When you have limited time to reach a conclusion and limited resources to attack the problem, you have to figure out which analyses are indispensable and which are simply gravy. As one of your first steps in designing your analysis, you should therefore figure out what *not* to do. This is the corollary of letting your hypothesis determine your analysis: avoiding analyses that don't relate to your hypothesis.

This holds especially true for small businesses with limited resources. They can't afford to boil the ocean, as Bob Buchsbaum, CEO of art supplies retailer Dick Blick Holdings, attests in describing his decision-making process:

> Look for the path of least resistance by being hypothesis driven; make assumptions and get answers that are "direction-

ally correct." We had a saying, "There is never enough data or enough time," which I always interpreted as, "Take action earlier rather than later." With a small business—$90 million in revenue—I can't let myself or my staff violate these lessons. Over and over, I find myself stopping people from building the "unifying theory" of the business.

As we discussed in the previous section, analytically minded people face a great temptation to do analyses that are interesting, rather than relevant. In designing your analysis plan, it is your responsibility to curtail this tendency in your team and, most especially, in yourself.

As your next step, you should figure out which analyses are quick wins—easy to complete and likely to make a major contribution to proving or refuting the initial hypothesis. In other words, as we say in Chapter 7, pluck the low-hanging fruit. As an example of how to think about this, Chacko Sonny of Savage Entertainment describes how his team attacks debugging, a crucial step in the development of any software product:

> Quality assurance for software in the early stages of testing is definitely centered on this principle. While we have to be exhaustive when searching for bugs in our software, and we can't afford to have 20 percent of the bugs slip through into a released product, the 80/20 rule* does apply when searching for the cause of a bug. In many cases, the same error in the code will cause a number of different symptoms. Rather than tracking down every single incarnation of the error, we will uncover 80 percent of the effects of a major bug. This will offer clues as to the cause of the errors. We can address a large problem in the code without having enumerated

*We will discuss the 80/20 rule at length in Chapter 4.

> every single effect of the bug. Early on, we try to catch the critical bugs with widespread implications for the product. Toward the end of the process, we catch the remaining 20 percent of issues, which allows us to tweak the product into releasable form.

By avoiding unnecessary analyses and focusing first on the easy wins, you put yourself in a position to get a lot done in a short time.

Forget about absolute precision. Because we stress the importance of fact-based analyses in making business decisions, you might think we're contradicting ourselves to say that you don't need precise answers from your analyses. The truth is, however, that business, for the most part, is not an exact discipline like physics or math. Deciding whether to open a new factory requires a different level of precision than discovering a new subatomic particle. In fact, in most situations, achieving a scientific level of exactitude for your management decisions is counterproductive. You will spend an inordinate amount of time and effort getting from mostly right to, in all likelihood, precisely wrong. Bear this in mind when determining the analysis tasks for your problem.

This is especially true with forward-looking analysis. It's one thing to assemble historical data to answer a question such as "How large is the widget market?" It's quite another to answer a question like "What is the likely return over the next 10 years if we build a new widget plant in Upper Sandusky?" The answer to that question depends on a great many variables, the values of which it is impossible to know: future widget demand, arrival of new competitors, changing consumer tastes, etc. Any number that you can come up with will most likely be wrong. Therefore, you should just try to get an answer that is in the "comfort zone"—directionally correct and of the right order of magnitude. Often you can reach an answer of that level of precision very quickly, while attaining spurious precision would take much longer.

Also, if you can achieve some sort of satisfactory answer in a short time, then you are much more likely to attempt the analysis than you would if you had to get an answer to four decimal places. As one of our alumni puts it:

> I find back-of-the-envelope analysis incredibly valuable because it lets you know if you're in the ballpark. A lot of the time, all I want to know is whether, say, a new product idea is going to be worth $5 million, $50 million, or $500 million. And some people find it very difficult to get comfortable with that. They think, "Oh, I'm going to say $50 million; what if it's really $75 million?" I don't care! "But it's 50 percent off!" they say. I respond that it's so much more valuable than not putting together a number at all.

Just as some people want to do every analysis under the sun, there are people who just have to get their answers correct to four significant figures. Naras Eechambadi, founder and CEO of Quaero, Inc., an information-based marketing consultancy, knows all about that from the inside:

> I hire a lot of Ph.D.s and advanced-degree holders, and I almost have to force them not to look at every error pattern in the data. All that stuff your professors taught you is great if you're talking about health care and you have to worry about people dying. But this is marketing; we're just trying to make a buck. Let's get the show on the road and stop worrying about all the nuances.
>
> You can spend a lot of time improving the precision of your models, but eventually you reach the point of diminishing returns or you lose time to market. We don't need to

> have the perfect model. We just need to have something that's better than what we have today. Let's go out and make some money, and then we can continue to make it better over time.

Once again, it is up to you to resist the impulse to get lost in the data, whether in yourself or your team, because it will cost you time and money.

Triangulate around the tough problems. In surveying and mapmaking, triangulation is the method of determining the precise location of an unknown point by taking measurements from two known points. You can use an analogous technique to form a hypothesis when you have very little information about the problem at hand—a very common occurrence in business. At some point you will come up against a question that appears unanswerable. Either the data are proprietary to your fiercest competitor, or you're breaking entirely new ground in your industry, or for whatever reason the question is just too tough to crack. If that's the case, don't despair. Chances are you can come up with some analyses that will at least allow you to scope out the likely limits of the answer, even if they won't get you particularly close. Once again, if you're directionally correct and in the right order of magnitude, chances are that's enough to make a decision.

To illustrate how this might be done, we'd like to present an example from our alumnus at GlaxoSmithKline, Paul Kenny. He had to determine the potential market size for a drug that had yet to be developed and that treats a condition most doctors don't even recognize. His strategy gives an insight into how you might tackle a similar situation:

> We're looking into a condition called hypoactive sexual desire disorder (HSDD), which is an abnormally low level of sexual desire, primarily in women. At this point, it's not

> really an accepted disease. It's been defined by psychiatrists but is very rarely diagnosed; GPs have probably never even heard of it. From a pharmaceutical point of view, it opens up the opportunity for some sort of female Viagra. At this point, there's no information on it.

Undaunted by this difficult scenario, Paul looked for analogous situations that might shed light on his problem:

> We've tried to draw some parallels with Viagra for men as an obvious link. Mainly, however, we're looking for analogies both with other sexual disorders and with what one might call lifestyle issues—obesity, say, or other diseases. We may be able to use these analogies to justify the business case.

Once Paul found some useful analogies, he looked for insights from them:

> One of the links we're hypothesizing is resistance—reluctance among patients to admit they have this condition. How many patients are actually going to talk to their doctor about it? At the moment, none of them do, so you can't use their history as an example. Of course, pre-Viagra, far fewer men talked to their doctor about ED [erectile dysfunction]. Whether women have the same attitude as men toward this remains an open question. On the mental side we're looking at obesity—patients have cravings, or they eat because it is a habit, or they think they want to, so that's more of a mental phenomenon—and the extent to which people admit they have obesity as a mental disease. There are all sorts of analogies that we're using to triangulate what sort of numbers we might be looking at. Even if, at the end of the day, we'll never know precisely, we hope to be able to come up with something in the ballpark.

As you can see, Paul's not in the least concerned that he will never reach "the answer." Rather, he's merely trying to establish upper and lower bounds for the size of this particular market, because that range will be enough for him to decide whether to pursue this project.

IMPLEMENTATION GUIDANCE

When designing your analysis, you have a specific end product in mind: your work plan. A comprehensive work plan begins with all the issues and subissues you identified during the framing of your initial hypothesis. For each issue or subissue, you should list the following elements:

- Your initial hypothesis as to the answer
- The analyses that must be done to prove or disprove that hypothesis, in order of priority
- The data necessary to perform the analysis
- The likely sources of the data (e.g., Census data, focus groups, interviews)
- A *brief* description of the likely end product of each analysis
- The person responsible for each end product (you or a member of your team)
- The due date for each end product

It doesn't need to be fancy or formal. Hand-drawn is fine, as long as it's legible.

As an example, let's return once more to Acme Widgets. When we left your team there in the last chapter, you had just finished your issue tree. We spent some time expanding one of the branches of that tree—the issue of "Can we implement the necessary changes?"—by dividing that issue into subissues expressed as yes/no questions. Table 2-1 shows how you could lay out the work plan for one of those subissues.

Table 2-1. Work Plan for Issue in Acme Widgets Issue Tree

Issue/Hypothesis	Analyses	Data Sources	End Product	Responsibility	Due Date
Can we implement the necessary changes to the production process? **Yes**					
Does the new process require special facilties? **No**	Technical Specifications	Articles, interviews	Chart	Tom	3-Jun
	List of facilities that meet new criteria	Facilities management, interviews	List	Tom	5-Jun
If it does require special facilities, can we acquire them? **Yes**	Map of "facilities gap"	Facilities management, thrum-mat line supervisors, interviews	Chart	Belinda	7-Jun
	Sources of required facilities/equipment	Operations, trade publications	List	Belinda	7-Jun
	Costs to fill gaps	Operations, contractors, interviews	Table	Belinda	10-Jun
	Effect on project rate of return	Finance department, prior analysis	Spreadsheet	Terry	12-Jun

Following the preceding list of elements in the analysis design, we start by noting the issue to be analyzed and our hypothesis as to the answer. We like to append our answer directly to the question, although you could just as easily put it in a separate column. The top-line issue goes (no surprise here) at the top. Beneath that, indent and list the subissues, then do the same with sub-subissues (not to mention sub-sub-subissues). Thus, the question "If it does require special facilities, can we acquire them?" comes underneath the question "Does the new process require special facilities?"

Next comes the list of analyses to be performed. In this example, there aren't many, but there could have been. For instance, it might be useful to have a schematic diagram to go along with the technical requirements for the new production process. Useful, yes, even interesting, but not ultimately necessary, and someone would have to take the time to put it together—time they wouldn't spend on actually proving or disproving the hypothesis. Therefore, doing a schematic didn't make the final cut, nor did a number of other analyses that you might devise.

We'll touch only briefly on the data and their sources, since we will be covering that topic in detail in Chapter 3. Listing data and sources helps you and your team cover all the bases so you will be less likely to miss a rich source of information. Speaking of rich sources of information, have you noticed how often interviews come up? You'll see a lot more about them in Chapter 3.

The description of the likely end product should be brief, as in the example. These descriptions really serve as a departure point for discussions within the team. At McKinsey, the EM takes each team member through her part of the work plan and discusses her expectations as to the end product. Sometimes, the EM will sketch out a "ghost pack," showing templates for each end product, which can help guide the analytical process, especially for less-experienced consultants.

Responsibility is mostly self-evident. After all, someone has to take charge of each analysis, or it won't get done. We'll cover the question of how you assign the right people to the right tasks (and get them on your team in the first place) in Chapter 6, "Managing Your Team." Usually, it makes sense to parcel out responsibility for discrete chunks of the analysis (e.g., for each subissue) to one person, but it's not a requirement. Thus, in our example, Tom is in charge of answering the question "Does the new process require special facilities?" Belinda is on the hook for finding out whether we can acquire any special facilities that we might need, but one piece of that analysis goes to Terry. Why? As it happens, Terry is our financial expert and is building an overall financial model for the project, so it makes sense for Terry to analyze the rate of return.

Due date, once again, is self-explanatory. Being specific about dates helps the members of your team understand what is expected of them and allows you to visualize the overall flow of the project from start to finish. Some people like to track their due dates in more detail with Gantt charts or other project management tools. That's up to you.

In our example, one analysis more or less dovetails neatly with the next. Bear in mind, however, that sometimes the results of one analysis will make a whole range of subsequent analyses redundant, thus saving you the trouble of actually performing them. For instance, if the analyses prove our initial hypothesis that we don't need special facilities, then the question of whether we can acquire them—and all the attendant analyses—falls away. Thus, if you can, you should schedule your analyses to let you answer these "dominant" questions first. Of course, sometimes you don't have the luxury to wait for the results of one analysis before you start the next. Still, make the most of opportunities to prune your analysis plan aggressively.

Beyond laying out your life for the next several weeks and setting expectations for your team, a good work plan has another feature: it helps you structure your thinking. As you go through your work plan, write down all the analyses, and prioritize and prune them, you'll quickly see whether there are holes in your initial hypothesis that didn't show up during the framing stage. One of our alumni put it this way:

> One of the most important things I've learned is that he who puts it on paper first wins. And the corollary is that if you can't put it down on paper, then either you don't have it clear in your head or it's not a good idea. There are a lot of people who say, "Oh, I had this idea in my head, I just haven't put it down, but I really know exactly what I want to do." I say, put it on paper.

Sometimes, just the process of work planning will lead you to revisit and possibly restructure your analysis. We will examine the iterative relationship between hypothesis and analysis more in Chapter 4. In the meantime, bear in mind that your initial hypothesis is a living document, and it feeds off your analysis.

EXERCISES

- In Chapter 1, we laid out part of the Acme Widgets issue tree regarding the question "Can we implement the necessary changes to utilize the new process?" In this chapter, we laid out a work plan for the subissue "Does it require special facilities that we don't have?" Do the same for the other subissue in that discussion, "Does it require special skills that we don't have?" Remember that if the answer is yes, you have to answer an additional question.

CONCLUSION

When it comes time to prove your initial hypothesis, efficient analysis design will help you hit the ground running. You and your team will know what you have to do, where to get the information to do it, and when to get it done. The work-planning process also serves as a useful reality check to the sometimes intellectualized pursuit of the initial hypothesis. To some, it may seem a slightly anal-retentive exercise, but we recommend it highly, and our alumni can attest to its utility.

Once you've designed your work plan, it's time to start filling in the blanks. You can only do that with facts, so it's time to start gathering data. In the next chapter, we'll take you through the strategies and techniques you need to get the data for your analysis.

3

GATHERING THE DATA

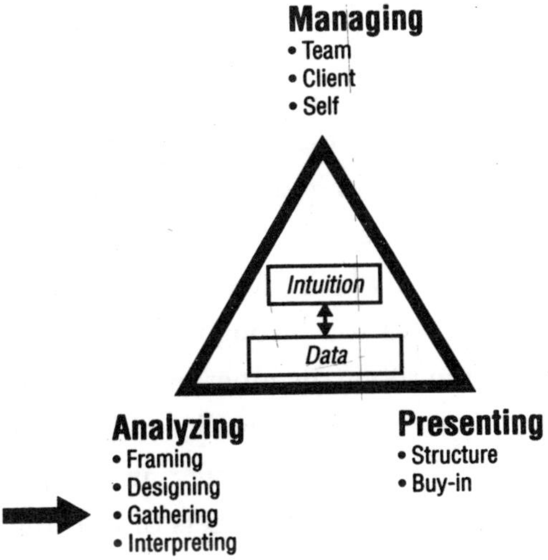

After developing your initial hypothesis and determining the analyses you need to prove it comes the unglamorous but all-important task of gathering the data necessary to perform those analyses. An unquenchable appetite for facts is one of the hallmarks of consulting à la McKinsey, and data gathering ranks among the most important consulting skills—just ask any new consultant after about six months on the job. Our interviews with

McKinsey alumni suggest that this area is also one of the most significant opportunities for improvement in other organizations. As described in our model in the introduction of this book, we suggest a balance between fact-based analysis and intuition. The key, however, is balance. Our hypothesis is that much of the daily decision making in business lacks rigorous, fact-based support, a McKinsey imperative and obsession since the Firm's founding in 1923.

In this chapter, we dive deep into the exciting world of data gathering. We begin, in the first section, with an overview of *research strategies*. We also share some successful techniques for conducting meaningful research—"gathering data smart" as one of our alumni put it. We get to the nitty-gritty with specific research tools widely recognized as best practices in and beyond McKinsey. Although some of these tools may sound familiar, their successful implementation with limited resources presents a constant challenge. The first section also identifies some of the best sources for data gathering, many of which are available free.

The second section takes you through one of McKinsey's most important data collection tools, the interview. A few incisive interview secrets can greatly improve the quality of your decision making. Follow our tried and tested techniques, and you'll boost your chances of uncovering those choice nuggets of information.

Finally, we've included a section on *knowledge management* (KM), one of the hottest current topics in business. In addition to describing effective KM strategies and tools, we share stories of how McKinsey alumni have successfully transformed KM efforts in their post-McKinsey organizations.

We considered writing a section on how to make research fun but lacked sufficient fact-based support. So we just focused on how to conduct it as painlessly as possible.

RESEARCH STRATEGIES AND TOOLS

As with most of the ideas in this book, we suggest taking a step back and thinking before jumping in. Let's face it, information availability is not the issue these days. Quite the opposite: we have too much of it. Our alumnus at GlaxoSmithKline, Paul Kenny, faces this problem every day:

> The data-gathering process has changed. I find loads of information on the Web, much more than even a few years ago. In pharmaceuticals, there is no shortage of data or information. In fact, we're inundated by it. There's information on the market, in very detailed form, along with a tremendous amount of complex scientific data. The difficulty is pinpointing the useful bits.

Rainer Siggelkow, owner and board member of US Forty and Bordercross Marketing, reiterates the need for strategic focus: "In our business, it is helpful to get to the one or two really important numbers that need to be considered. There isn't time for more." We concur. When doing your research, you don't want to get as much information as possible, you want to get the most important information as quickly as possible.

As illustrated by the previous two alumni quotes, McKinsey's dedication to strategic fact-finding has a place in other organizations as well. Have you ever been involved in a data search that took forever yet yielded little? That's what we hope to avoid. Let's review how McKinsey gathers data and then discuss new lessons learned as these concepts are implemented in other organizations.

THE McKINSEY WAY

Let's briefly review McKinsey's principles for research:

Facts are friendly. Problem solving at McKinsey relies on facts. Facts compensate for a consultant's lack of experience and intuition relative to an executive with years of business experience. Facts also bridge the credibility gap between consultant and client; they allow the consultant to show she knows her stuff. Despite (or possibly because of) the power of facts, many businesspeople fear them, but hiding from unpleasant facts will, at best, delay the inevitable.

Don't accept "I have no idea." People always have an idea if you probe a bit. Ask a few pointed questions, and you'll be amazed at what people know. If you ask someone a question and the person responds, "I have no idea," treat it as a challenge. Chances are, the response stems from a lack of time, a feeling of insecurity, or worst of all, sheer idleness. Your challenge is to figure out the source of resistance and adjust accordingly.

Remember, too, that just as you shouldn't accept "I have no idea" from others, so you shouldn't accept it from yourself. With a bit of thinking and searching, you'll usually find that you do know something, or at least can find it out.

Specific research tips. Three high-impact techniques courtesy of McKinsey to enhance your research are (1) start with the annual report, (2) look for outliers, and (3) look for best practices. The annual report offers a wealth of information about a company in one package; be sure to read the message to the shareholders or CEO's report. Outliers analysis (often accomplished with the help of a computer) is a tool to isolate key opportunities for investigation within a firm. This method involves comparing ratios or calculating key measures (such as sales per salesperson by region), paying particular attention to high and low performers. Finally, although the term *best practices* may be painfully familiar (as one of the business buzzwords of the 1990s), most companies can still learn from a competitor or other top-performing organization, even one in a different industry.

LESSONS LEARNED AND IMPLEMENTATION ILLUSTRATIONS

How can you take the McKinsey lessons of strategic data gathering and apply them in your organization? Our interviews with McKinsey alumni who have worked to transfer the data orientation and fact-finding approaches to post-McKinsey organizations helped us identify three ways to get this done:

- Diagnose the data orientation of your organization.
- Demonstrate the power of good facts.
- Build the proper infrastructure.

Diagnose the data orientation of your organization. The cultures of organizations vary widely, as do their "data orientations." McKinsey has developed a strong, fact-based culture that mandates factual support for articulated positions, both in internal communications to employees and in external communications to clients. When they leave the Firm, many alumni are surprised at the lack of concrete data analysis in their new organizations. Stevie McNeal, vice president at Blue Cross/Blue Shield of North Carolina, identified the absence of facts as a potential inhibitor of effective decision making. "Certain facts and the effective communication thereof can be intimidating," she observes, "especially when people are operating without a basis in facts and logic."

A fact-oriented culture is hardly the exclusive preserve of McKinsey, however. Other companies can and do rely on data ahead of instinct, and some McKinsey alumni have helped their organizations develop this attitude. The first step in advancing data collection efforts in your organization is to assess your particular situation honestly. Is the culture in your company more or less fact based? Do colleagues present their ideas with factual support? Do the decision makers explain the basis of their choices with reference to evidence? Naturally, there will be variance within the organization, but you shouldn't take long to diagnose the dominant orientation, if you can't pinpoint it already.

Once you've analyzed your organization, you can begin redressing any imbalances that you discover, particularly the aspects you can control. Start within your sphere of influence—your direct reports and department. If necessary, take a grassroots approach to spreading the word. Of course, if you have the luxury of building a department or company from scratch, you can start from a fact-based orientation. Before you can determine the right balance for your organization, however, you need to follow the ancient maxim "Know thyself."

Demonstrate the power of good facts. Dan Veto left McKinsey to form the strategic planning group of the huge conglomerate Conseco. He used his skill at gathering, synthesizing, and communicating facts to earn the respect of his internal clients, the division presidents:

> I was new to the organization and in charge of building credibility for a newly created group within the company. I wanted to make the new strategy group contribute to the overall company's success as quickly as possible. It took a couple of months, but I was able to establish critical, credible relationships with the SBU [strategic business unit] heads, who are, in essence, our clients. My strategy, based on my McKinsey experiences, was to have our team focus on providing fact-based insights using information that previously had not been shared among the business units.

By devoting more thought and attention to data gathering, you will be able to generate credible insights you might not otherwise reach—and with the fact base, your insights will be credible. By relying more on facts, you should be able to increase the impact of your analyses and recommendations within your organization. Use Dan's example, and spread the word on the power of fact-based insights.

Build the proper infrastructure. McKinsey has the luxury of abundant resources for data gathering. In addition to the extensive databases that codify all studies and expertise within the Firm, McKinsey employs information specialists, who run office libraries and assist consultants in their data gathering. Lists of studies, names of experts, "sanitized"* reports, industry studies, and Wall Street analyst reports reach a consultant's desk on the first day of a new study. The consultant receives not just lots of information, but the right information.

A former McKinsey-ite who is now an executive at a major financial institution recognizes that most companies' data support efforts don't reach the bar set by McKinsey:

> I find that most companies do very little in this regard, and their efforts are very spread out. We have a corporate library, but I miss the value of conversation with an expert who understands business and knows exactly how to point me in the right direction.

We won't venture an estimate of the exact budget needed for data collection activities. Suffice it to say that you should probably spend more than whatever you currently are spending. At McKinsey, consultants rely on internal reports, industry reports,

*Sanitized reports are client documents that have been modified for sharing within the Firm. To ensure confidentiality, client names are eliminated from sanitized reports, and financial or other data are disguised.

analyst reports, census data, and the like. Identify the key data sources for the kind of information most important to your particular organization, and spend whatever is necessary to secure these sources—within the constraints of your oganization's budget, of course.

IMPLEMENTATION GUIDANCE

Strategic data gathering can significantly improve your effectiveness and efficiency. Perhaps a (hypothetical) nonbusiness example will help bring the point home.

Jerry and Marilyn want to buy a new car. Jerry sees an advertisement on TV for a new SUV from Honda. He likes the way it looks and knows from experience that Honda makes quality automobiles. He goes out the next day to the dealer, sees a color that he knows Marilyn likes, and orders the car. It will arrive in two weeks.

Marilyn has a hunch that Jerry is moving too quickly on the car purchase as he often relies on his intuition to guide his actions. Being a bit more fact-oriented, she ponders her situation and decides to do a little research. She logs on to her new fast-access Internet connection that her son helped her install the weekend before and begins gathering data and accessing consumer reports (see Appendix A for similar leads).

Once she has compared features and statistics for the various models (utilizing key decision criteria such as room for grandkids, safety, and fuel efficiency), she changes gears. She then gathers some information about different fishing rod and reel combinations because she knows Jerry is thinking about buying new equipment for the annual family trip to the lake. She prints out some excellent, brief comparison reports on different fishing sets, including price data, from four different manufacturers. Jerry is impressed by the rod and reel information and together they make the purchase online. Two days later he asks whether or not Marilyn has considered making similar comparisons for the auto purchase they're planning.

As you consider the potential impact of powerful facts in your organization, try out this method, just as Marilyn did, and seek to provide insights not previously available (the goal of effective data gathering). Based on your company's primary objectives, such as profitability and sales growth, take the time to find out what is important. Then gather the right facts and share the insights.

When it comes to building a more fact-based culture, don't try to go at it alone. McKinsey did not achieve its research expertise without adequate, dedicated resources. Make the investment to hire research specialists, and grant full authority to purchase the right journals and reports that will prove useful to decision making in the organization. Be selective, however. Monitor their use to control spending, and evaluate their usefulness. This strategy will vary with the specifics of your organization, of course. A large multinational will have the need and ability to build a more sophisticated support structure than a five-person start-up. Remember that you need more than just a budget; you also need the right cultural elements, including the incentives to increase the usage of facts in your organization. We will discuss this issue in more detail in the knowledge management section of this chapter.

Finally, given the importance of "good" data sources, we have included a summary of some of the outstanding research tools currently available to the public. Table 3-1 (pages 58–59) lists some powerful search engines and general information guides. In addition, Appendix A provides a long list of the most helpful data sources we could find.* Some of these sources contain a lot of general information (e.g., Census Bureau data), while others focus on

*Special thanks to David Ernsthausen, information specialist at the Kenan-Flagler School of Business at the University of North Carolina at Chapel Hill, who assisted in this compilation. Note that although these sources were accurate at the time of writing, Web addresses and contents can change rapidly.

Table 3-1. Selected Public Data Sources

Category	Name	Description	Cost	Location
Search engines	Asianet's Select Search Engines	Over 950 search engines in one place	Free	www.asianet.net/search.html
Search engines	Findspot	Nice search engine guide plus search assistance	Free	www.findspot.com
Search engines	Google	Easy search that claims access to over 1.3 billion Web pages	Free	www.google.com
Search engines	Hotbot	Full text of over 100 million Web pages	Free	www.hotbot.lycos.com
Search engines	Alta Vista	Power search engine—especially for advanced searches	Free	www.altavista.com
Search engines	FAST Search	Claims access to over 575 million URLs; extensive list of sites	Free	www.alltheweb.com
Search engines	Yahoo	One of the old standards—some commercialization	Free	www.yahoo.com
Search engines	BPubs.com	Allows searches just on business publications	Free	www.bpubs.com

Category	Name	Description	Cost	Location
General information	ABI/Inform Global (Proquest Direct)	Abstracts and some full text for articles in over 1,000 leading journals	Varies	Subscription information at www.proquest.com
General information	Academic Universe (Lexis/Nexis)	General and specific industry and company information; major news wires	Varies	Subscription information at www.lexis-nexis.com
General information	AJR NewsLink	Access to over 3,400 U.S. and 2,000 non–U.S. newspapers	Free	ajr.newslink.org/news.html
General information	Business & Industry	Facts, figures, and key events for international companies	Varies	Subscription information at www.galegroup.com/welcome.html
General information	Business Wire	Business news and information about industries and companies—latest news	Free	www.businesswire.com
General information	Dow Jones Interactive	Extensive access to full-text articles from newspapers, magazines, journals, and broadcast media	Varies	Subscription information at http://askdj.dowjones.com/
General information	Individual.com	Free company and industry news; can be customized based on your input	Free	www.individual.com

specific subjects or industries. Experiment with them a bit, and you'll soon discover which sources can provide you with the "right" information in the easiest fashion. And remember, quality over quantity.

EXERCISES

- Conduct a data orientation audit. Obtain the material from your last big presentation (to your board, boss, spouse, etc.), and review the written material and notes. Summarize the key arguments. Under each argument, jot down the facts that support the points. How many facts do you have? Do you make any arguments without supporting facts? If so, this is a red flag. Depending upon the nature of the presentation, you should have at least three good supporting facts for each point (unless one fact is a slam dunk).
- Develop a data-gathering plan for a current problem. What major issue at work keeps you up at night? Analyze it. First, develop your overall hypothesis (from Chapter 1). Then think of at least three major arguments, and identify the most relevant fact or two that may support the position (or disprove it). Next, identify the potential source of the information (document or person). You may have to get creative here.

INTERVIEWING

We didn't have to look far for an example to illustrate the importance of interviewing in non-McKinsey positions. In writing this book, we used interviewing as our primary data collection method and found the interviewing techniques we learned at the Firm extremely helpful. In conducting interviews with dozens of McKinsey alumni and sending E-mail questionnaires to thousands of alumni, we focused on identifying the right people, carefully thinking through our interview guides and questionnaires, and diligently documenting our findings. We then summarized the content of the interviews on spreadsheets and used our alumni's comments throughout the book.

The Firm relies extensively on interviews. In fact, interviewing is part of every McKinsey engagement, as it not only generates primary data but can also identify great sources of secondary data. The value of interviewing also extends beyond data gathering by serving as a mechanism to test ideas and increase buy-in (see Chapter 7). Let's review some interviewing tips from McKinsey and identify how you can successfully implement specific interview techniques in your organization.

THE McKINSEY WAY

In interviewing, McKinsey emphasizes preparation and courtesy.

Be prepared: write an interview guide. An interview guide is simply a written list of the questions you want to ask, arranged in the order you expect to ask them. There are two reasons why you should have such a guide. First, placing your thoughts on paper forces you to organize them. Second, the guide helps the interviewee to identify the topics you intend to cover in the interview and prepare accordingly.

Your guide should be brief. Boil down your list of questions to the three or four most important. Your goal should be to get those answered in the limited time you have with the interviewee; anything more is gravy. And don't forget to close with every

McKinsey-ite's favorite question: "Is there anything I forgot to ask?" Every now and then, it hits pay dirt.

When conducting interviews, listen and guide. Conduct your interviews in a rigorous but sensitive manner. Active listening—acknowledging the interviewee with nods, interjections, and the "McKinsey grunt" ("uh-huh, uh-huh")—plays a key part in that, but don't overlook the value of silence. Use positive body language. Don't let the interviewee lead you off on tangents or, worse, the garden path; politely but firmly keep the interviewee on track.

Seven tips for successful interviews. McKinsey consultants have many stratagems for conducting effective interviews:

1. Have the interviewee's boss set up the meeting.
2. Interview in pairs.
3. Listen, don't lead.
4. Paraphrase, paraphrase, paraphrase.
5. Use the indirect approach.
6. Don't ask for too much.
7. Adopt the Columbo tactic.

Most of these are self-explanatory, save the last one. Lieutenant Columbo was a 1970s TV cop played by Peter Falk. He would often finish questioning a suspect and then pause by the door to ask one more question—usually a zinger. This tactic succeeded because the suspects often dropped their guard and allowed the truth to come out. You can try this approach if you think an interviewee is holding out on you. Who knows, you just might crack the case.

Don't leave the interviewee naked. Some people become uncomfortable under the stress of an interview. As the interviewer, you are responsible for being sensitive to the fears of the interviewee. Establish a connection with him in order to get those few bits of information you seek. Don't squeeze the interviewee dry and leave him regretting the process afterward. Instead, take time to explain the positive impact the information may make and the primary objectives of your time together, and give some good information in return as a quid pro quo. As the interviewer, you often occupy a position of power relative to the interviewee; you have a responsibility to use that power wisely.

Difficult interviews. No matter how well prepared and sensitive you are, you will eventually face someone who is just a "difficult" interviewee. This person may have his own ideas of how things should be, and they definitely don't match up with yours. If an interviewee is playing hardball, you may have to as well—just hope his bat isn't a lot bigger than yours.

This person could be the "sandbagger," an individual who purposely withholds key information. A sandbag is just an obstacle to go around, so your path of least resistance should lead you to another source for the information you need. Of course, if you have the right heavy equipment, you can just bulldoze her out of the way.

The most difficult interviewee, though, is the person whose job is truly threatened by the problem-solving process. The person is likely to get fired, and you know it. Unfortunately, there's no easy way around this one; you just have to soldier on for the benefit of the organization as a whole.

Always write a thank-you note. Writing thank-you notes is not just good etiquette; this is good business. Thank-you letters can really help in building a relationship that can yield future benefits. Imagine the nice feeling you get when you receive an unexpected thank-you letter. Many of us need to fight the temptation to neglect this courtesy because we keep moving forward at such a rapid pace, especially in the wired and wireless world of the New Economy. Take time to smell the roses, and thank someone for them as well.

LESSONS LEARNED AND IMPLEMENTATION ILLUSTRATIONS

You may not think about it explicitly, but you probably interview someone every day. It could be a customer, coworker, or competitor. Consider how many times you have interacted with someone who had important data and information that related to a problem you were working on. What, after all, is interviewing? Nothing more than a discussion between two or more persons conducted for the purpose of gaining specific information and usually with a slightly higher than normal level of formality.

Consultants, especially consultants at McKinsey, treat interviews with the utmost respect. They spend much time and effort preparing for them and learning from them. You should, too.

Our discussions with McKinsey alumni confirmed the effectiveness of interviewing skills when transferred to other organizations. Outside the Firm, however, the context is different. McKinsey interviews are a standard operating procedure for every project, and they are conducted with purposeful consistency (to the extreme of having a specific MS Word template for summarizing findings). In other business scenarios, interviews are regarded differently. As a result, they are often less formal, with much less preparation and follow-through. Our alumni told us stories of how they have been working to increase the effectiveness of data gathering through interviews, and they helped us identify ways you can make the most of interviewing in your career:

- Structure your interviews.
- Interviewing is about listening.
- Be sensitive.

Structure your interviews. You may have sensed by now that we subscribe to the logical, ordered, and structured approach to problem solving. This orientation is probably a combination of our upbringing, personalities, and training at McKinsey. Since we both left the Firm, we have come to appreciate a little variety in our working environments, particularly the difference in levels of formality. Nevertheless, when it comes to interviewing, even in less formal situations, we highly recommend sticking to the structure and basic rules described earlier, beginning with interview guides. One alumna now at a major financial institution emphatically concurs:

> I always have interview guides—always—whether I'm talking to people internally or meeting with people externally. I usually refer to [my guide] for the four or five high-level questions I want to explore. I think it's very important to figure out what I am trying to get at before I go in.

Although the context of interviews (the relationship, objectives, and tone) can vary considerably, certain elements remain the same. McKinsey consultants absorb this message early and learn to use the same format time after time (if it ain't broke, don't fix it). In truth, you don't have to develop anything elaborate or time-consuming.

We have included copies of the interview guides we used for our data collection effort for this book. In our situation, we developed two interview guides, one for E-mail questionnaires that we sent to thousands of McKinsey alumni and one for the dozens of in-person interviews we conducted. Our primary goal for the E-mail questionnaires (Figure 3-1, pages 66–67) was to guide the respondents to hit the major areas of our outline and to share war stories from their post-McKinsey experiences. Notice that it is a bit longer and more specific than the in-person interview guide. We also sent a nice cover letter introducing ourselves, describing the project, and identifying our key objectives. The in-person interview guide (Figure 3-2, page 68) followed the same general format but

Figure 3-1. *The McKinsey Mind* E-Mail Questionnaire

Thank you for taking the time to complete this questionnaire. Please return your answers via E-mail to Paul Friga.

What is your name, company (if any), and position or function? ____________

____

What is the most important lesson that you learned at McKinsey? How does it affect the way you work in your current position? ____________

____

In the following items, we have laid out a set of categories that summarizes the tools many of us learned at the Firm. For each, please think about what you learned at the Firm with regard to each category and give an example of how you've applied it in your post-McKinsey experience. ____________

____

Framing the Problem: The skills and techniques that allow McKinsey-ites to break apart problems, e.g., initial hypotheses, brainstorming, and analytical frameworks from previous engagements. ____________

____

Gathering the Data: The techniques used to gather and manage data to test hypotheses, e.g., interviewing, PD searches. ____________

____

Analyzing the Data: The methods McKinsey uses to extract useful conclusions from the data. This category includes such favorites as "80/20" and "Don't boil the ocean." ____________

____

Presenting Your Ideas: Techniques and tips for getting the message across, whether in a formal presentation with blue books or an informal meeting with client team members, e.g., "One message per chart," "the elevator test," and the ever-important prewiring. ____________

____

Managing Your Team: The skills McKinsey team leaders use (or sometimes don't) to keep their teams effective, including team selection, internal communications, and team bonding. ______________________

____

Managing Your Client: The ever-important process of keeping the client on your side. Includes selling the study, structuring the engagement, and managing client teams. ______________________

____

Managing Yourself: Life at McKinsey can be tough. Most of us managed to find some way of juggling life at the Firm with real life, e.g., managing expectations, managing our bosses, and managing our "significant others." ______

____

What problems have you faced in implementing McKinsey methods into your new organization? ______________________

____

Would you be interested and/or willing to conduct a short interview with us, either over the phone or in person? If so, please give us your contact numbers. ______________________

Is there a question about McKinsey we've forgotten to ask? What's your answer? ______________________

If we use any of the stories you send us in the book, we will send you a signed copy; we will also mention you in the acknowledgments unless you request anonymity. ______________________

Please list your (snail-) mailing address: ______________________

____

Do you wish to have your name disguised if we use any of your stories?
___Yes ___No

Do you want your name mentioned in the acknowledgments if we use one of your stories? ___Yes ___No

Figure 3-2. *The McKinsey Mind* In-Person Interview Guide

1. What is the most significant application of a particular tool or technique that you learned during your tenure at McKinsey in your new position? What was the context? How did it go?

2. In the following items, we have laid out a set of categories that summarizes the tools many of us learned at the Firm. For each, please try to give an example of how you've applied it in your post-McKinsey experience—include the particular tool/technique/strategy, context, application, reaction, and success.

Framing the Problem: The skills and techniques that allow McKinsey-ites to break apart problems, e.g., initial hypotheses, brainstorming, and analytical frameworks from previous engagements.

Gathering the Data: The techniques used to gather and manage data to test hypotheses, e.g., interviewing, PD searches.

Analyzing the Data: The methods McKinsey uses to extract useful conclusions from the data. This category includes such favorites as "80/20" and "Don't boil the ocean."

Presenting Your Ideas: Techniques and tips for getting the message across, whether in a formal presentation with blue books or an informal meeting with client team members, e.g., "One message per chart," "the elevator test," and the ever-important prewiring.

Managing Your Team: The skills McKinsey team leaders use (or sometimes don't) to keep their teams effective, including team selection, internal communications, and team bonding.

Managing Your Client: The ever-important process of keeping the client on your side. Includes selling the study, structuring the engagement, and managing client teams.

Managing Yourself: Life at McKinsey can be tough. Most of us managed to find some way of juggling life at the Firm with real life, e.g., managing expectations, managing our bosses, and managing our "significant others."

Is there a question about McKinsey we've forgotten to ask? What's your answer?

was a bit more open-ended and allowed the interviewee to move between the sections more freely. We tried, as much as possible, to simplify our message to emphasize the key points we wanted to cover. This made the interview go much more smoothly and kept us focused as well.

Unless you actually want to catch your interviewee off guard, you should share the interview guide with him ahead of time. Be sure to take notes during the interview, and write them up legibly afterward.

Interviewing is about listening. After leaving McKinsey in 1997, Dean Dorman spent a year working directly under Gary Leiver at GE, then moved to an E-commerce start-up. Now he is the president and chief operating officer of Silver Oak Partners, providing strategic sourcing services to the leveraged-buyout industry. Dean is one of the hardest-charging individuals you could ever meet and is never at a loss for words, but even Dean appreciates the importance of listening for today's business leaders:

> Before I took my position as president of Silver Oak, I served on the advisory board for about a year. During that time, I paid attention to management's plans. I also developed my own hypotheses of what needed to get done to take the company to the next level. My first task as president was to launch what I call the "look, listen, and learn" tour to test any hypotheses. Over the course of the first six weeks, I met with all the functional and initiative leaders and interviewed them for about two or three hours each. Taking the time early on to listen to people has proved invaluable. It has allowed me to have a real impact on the company.

When you are new to an organization, there are obvious benefits to listening just as Dean did, but listening isn't just for the new guy in the office. Effective managers spend a majority of their time listening. Unfortunately, our formal educational systems provide very little training in listening. Many of us learn the hard way. The key lessons from McKinsey that you can apply in your work situation are to recognize the importance of listening, increase the amount of time you spend listening (to the right people and on the right subjects), and listen in an active manner.

Active listening simply means encouraging and guiding the interviewee's responses through the effective use of verbal and nonverbal signals. Head nodding, arm crossing, and facial expressions play a bigger role in interviews than you think. If you are truly paying attention to the interview, these things should come naturally. If you feel that you are forcing them, perhaps the interview should have ended about 15 minutes earlier.

Be sensitive. In their efforts to implement interview techniques in their post-McKinsey positions, our McKinsey alumni learned that style matters. Some people (wrongly, in our view) see interviewees as a source of information to be drained dry. We suggest a different tack. Try to establish a connection with the interviewee. Treat the interview as a chance to meet a new person and actively involve her in the problem-solving effort. The interview is a two-way exchange that involves much more than a one-way information transfer. If you let the interviewee become your partner in the process, you will be able develop this relationship.

When it comes to the actual interview, the beginning matters. It sets the tone for the rest of your time with the interviewee. McKinsey consultants learn to avoid sensitive issues at the beginning. This requires some forethought in order to identify what may be "sensitive." For example, if you are working on a cost-cutting project that may involve layoffs, you might not want to start your questions with the number of years the person has been in that position and the exact nature of her contribution to the bottom line. Francesca Brockett, the senior vice president of strategic planning and business development at Toys "R" Us, has incorporated this thinking in her approach:

> I think the most important thing I learned at McKinsey related to interviewing is to start with less-sensitive issues. I have used this general technique frequently in developing relationships in my department and across the organization. It is probably part of my DNA at this point.

Bear in mind individual agendas as well. Everyone you encounter day to day—employees, customers, competitors—has an agenda. After all, an agenda is just a set of objectives that each person has and may hope to accomplish or expedite through you. There will be times when agendas conflict, and your job as the interviewer is to anticipate and plan for such situations. For instance, you may be able to help an interviewee accomplish his objective (provided it doesn't interfere with your goals). At the least, express empathy for the interviewee's situation, and avoid issues that may cause unnecessary friction.

IMPLEMENTATION GUIDANCE

Let's start our implementation ideas with a brief story about McKinsey consultants' training in people skills. The Firm sends every consultant who makes it through the first year to an Interpersonal Skills Workshop (ISW), usually in a beautiful rural setting in Germany or England. The leaders of this weeklong, intensive, and enlightening workshop carefully analyze each participant's ability to get along with others.

It was at one of these sessions, in Germany's majestic Black Forest, that one of the authors* had an eye-opening experience.

---

*Not Ethan; the other one.

Reflecting on his brief professional career, he realized that he was so focused on setting and accomplishing goals that the finished product had become an obsession. He had blinded himself to everything that lay between him and the end result; he had forgotten that there is not just the destination, there is also the journey. We believe that task completion must be balanced with process interaction; that means you should try to get things done without stepping on people as you go. So it is with interviewing; relationships matter. Think through your personal approach, and consider expanding your capabilities if necessary.

Think through your daily schedule, and identify all of the opportunities you have to obtain important information from people and how you should relate to those people. Do you prepare adequately to take full advantage of these opportunities? Do you document what you learn, so you won't forget it? As you think through your schedule, try to find more time to listen and less to speak.

After that recommendation, you might be hankering for something a bit less touchy-feely, a bit more concrete, so let's move on to the issue of structure. Earlier in this section, we discussed the interview guide and gave you some examples. Structure doesn't end with the development of an interview guide, however. There are two additional opportunities for "interview discipline": pre-interview communication and the post-interview follow-up.

You should send the interview guide (or a version of it) to the interviewee well ahead of the interview. If you send it more than a week in advance, it may make sense to resend the guide when you confirm the appointment. This allows the interviewee to prepare responses and identify additional support that may help you immensely. Interviewees will also appreciate the courtesy, because, let's face it, most of us don't like surprises. There are a few times to bend this rule, of course. For example, in politically charged situations, you might not want to allow for preparation that may facilitate resistance or deception. In general, however, this should be your standard operating procedure for interviews. One alumnus, now a senior administrator in the German government, elaborates on some of the benefits of sending the guides ahead of time and follow-up:

> I make extensive use of interviews during the early phases of projects to clarify hypotheses, identify relevant material needs, and create buy-in. We develop interview guides and send them in advance to allow the interviewees to prepare and track down information that they do not already have. After the interview, we document our findings and give that as feedback to the interviewee to make sure we understood him properly . . . and to correct any misunderstandings.

Post-interview follow-up also adds value to the interview process. It gives you a chance to confirm what you heard and to ensure you understood what was said. It is much better to have that clarification earlier in the process, as the error can magnify over time. (Remember those school-yard games of "telephone" in which a sentence gets whispered around a circle and emerges hilariously unrecognizable?) Don't forget to send the all-important and often-missed thank-you letters, as previously discussed.

Finally, on the topic of sensitivity, when it comes to starting the interview off on the right foot, start slowly and gently. It is usually safe to begin with a big picture of what you are trying to accomplish and why you are meeting with that particular person. Consider an icebreaker to get things moving, but avoid platitudes like "Nice weather, isn't it?" Rather, try to empathize with the interviewee and what she does. For instance, "I don't think I could ever spot defective widgets with my eyesight. How perfect does your vision have to be to do a job like yours?" As always, circumstances may require a different approach, but we recommend making a connection before you start pressing on sensitive subjects.

EXERCISES

- Develop an interview guide. First, identify your next big interview opportunity. Then list your objectives or the critical information you would like to obtain. (Work from your hypothesis, as discussed in Chapters 1 and 2). Now pare the list down. Combine where possible, and eliminate irrelevant points. You should end up with two or three primary objectives for the meeting. Next, structure the interview guide around those key questions. Don't forget to consider the interviewee's agenda and watch for sensitive issues. Send your interview guide to the interviewee at least two days in advance.
- Write a thank-you letter. Nothing complicated here, just a discipline exercise. Write a good old-fashioned handwritten or typed thank-you letter. If it feels good, write another one!

KNOWLEDGE MANAGEMENT

Ah, knowledge management (KM). It's one of the hottest business buzzwords today, and one of the least understood. According to a recent *Business Week* survey, more than 80 percent of 158 large multinational corporations already have or are actively developing formal knowledge management programs.* McKinsey has long been recognized as a leader in the field of KM and has much to offer other organizations as they formalize their KM efforts.

What is KM? First, we should tell you what knowledge is not—data and information. Data are facts, observations about

*Neil Gross. "Mining a Company's Mother Lode of Talent," *Business Week*, August 28, 2000, p. 135–137.

occurrences, and numbers. Information is a collection and some synthesis of data. Knowledge is the mix of information, experience, and context in a value-adding process. That process occurs first in the heads of individuals (where it is what we call "uncodified knowledge") and can be shared with others through discussions or documentation (at which point the knowledge becomes "codified"). KM is the systematic process by which an organization maximizes the value of the uncodified and codified knowledge in the firm. In general, this means the codified knowledge has been captured in databases or documents.

Many executives and academics focus their KM efforts on codification strategies, including technology platforms. We believe, and McKinsey teaches, that even the best KM technologies can capture only a small portion of the true knowledge in a firm. Therefore, a truly successful strategy must move beyond technology if it is to capture and distill the valuable experience that is walking around the hallways.

Bill Ross, a McKinsey alumnus now working for GE as the manager of business development for the Transportation Division, commented on KM in his new firm:

> I was fortunate to land at a company that values knowledge just as McKinsey did. GE is a learning organization, and the person in charge of that effort is Jack Welch. In fact, Jack will say that the KM ability of GE is the core element that has led the company to its great success.
>
> Everyone in the organization pays attention to best practices, inside and outside of the organization. There is regular communication between divisions and special groups, such as a services council, where we stay abreast of everyone's key projects. We don't try to do it through a massive database, as it would be too hard to keep updating. This is

real time and best done through regular get-togethers such as cross-group quarterly meetings to discuss best practices.

KM means taking advantage of what is known to maximize the firm's value. We believe this to be an important endeavor, and based on the time and effort it puts into KM, so does McKinsey. In this section, we briefly recap McKinsey's KM strategy and then share advice and stories about KM in other organizations.

THE McKINSEY WAY

The central KM-related principle at McKinsey is this: don't reinvent the wheel.

Don't reinvent the wheel. Whatever problem you're facing, chances are that someone, somewhere has worked on something similar. McKinsey recognizes the value of retaining and exploiting that experience, and the Firm goes to great lengths to codify it. The Firm maintains two primary databases. One, called PD-Net, includes previous reports generated and cleansed for sharing among the Firm's consultants. You could think of it as the "know what" database. The other database is a directory of all the Firm's experts in various industries and practice areas; call it the "know who" database. Users of either database can sort the data by industry, time, expert, office, and a number of other criteria.

LESSONS LEARNED AND IMPLEMENTATION ILLUSTRATIONS

McKinsey is in the business of selling knowledge, as are a lot of other companies. The challenge is how to take advantage of what is known in the firm, both uncodified and codified knowledge.

We view KM from a holistic perspective that goes beyond technology. We recommend using the schematic framework of the crit-

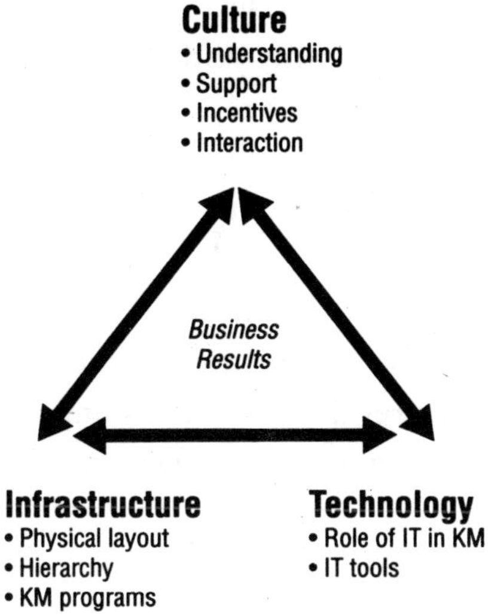

Source: "Knowledge Management in Research and Development," *Research and Technology Management* (July/August 2001).

Figure 3-3. Knowledge Management (KM) Enablers Framework

ical areas of KM* shown in Figure 3-3. Culture describes the way a company's employees understand KM, have support and incentives to share knowledge, and interact in a sharing, interdepartmental manner. At McKinsey, there is a well-understood KM strategy whereby knowledge sharing is expected of all employees and rewarded accordingly. The infrastructure pertains to the physical layout of offices and departments, organizational structure, and the KM program itself (including KM officers). As an example of KM infrastructure, McKinsey has an extensive network of information specialists in every office who can lend immediate assistance to teams trying to get up to speed on new areas and industries. Other organizations have begun dedicating similar

*This framework originally appeared in Armbrecht, Chapas, Chappelow, Farris, Friga, et al. "Knowledge Management in Research and Development," *Research and Technology Management* (July/August 2001), pp. 28–48.

resources to KM. Finally, the technology represents the specific strategies firms take to codify and share their knowledge most effectively. Corporate intranets represent one of the most common KM technology platforms. With any technology platform, keeping the information it contains current and high quality is an ongoing challenge. The center of the triangle includes the words *business results*, a reminder that the yardstick for any KM effort is its bottom-line impact on the organization. We used this framework to interpret the results from our alumni interviews and came up with the following lessons regarding KM implementation efforts:

- Develop a rapid-response culture.
- Acquire external knowledge.
- Control the quality of your input: garbage in, garbage out.

Develop a rapid-response culture. The culture of an organization is a tough beast to tame and extremely important. We define culture as a combination of the employees' shared values and assumptions regarding the organization and its events and processes, the organization's incentive programs, and the nature of daily interaction among employees. Examples would be the level of formality (e.g., use of first names, dress code), the exhibited level of respect between colleagues, and the amount of socializing. Another example, extremely important in KM systems and data gathering, is the rate at which employees respond to data requests from other employees. It is difficult to run an effective KM system without access to the uncodified knowledge in other people's heads. A rapid-response culture can help give you the most access.

Larry Rouvelas, the executive vice president of Pulse Medical Instruments, a small technology company, misses the McKinsey culture in this regard:

> At McKinsey, there is an ethic of response whereby if anyone—even the most junior consultant—makes a call to a colleague anywhere around the world, the call will be returned within 24 hours. This helps immensely with data collection as well as for general guidance. This is not the case in other organizations, although I am trying to develop that in my company.

Acquire external knowledge. Knowledge can be generated either internally or externally. Internal knowledge creation involves disseminating information to employees through discussions or documents, and it is a vital part of any KM strategy. External knowledge matters, too. As discussed earlier, McKinsey invests heavily in order to maintain access to the latest thinking inside and outside of the Firm. Every project starts with a search of internal documents as well as the identification of external publications or industry experts who might have something to contribute.

The same holds true at other organizations. Jack Welch doesn't hesitate to search for the best ideas from any external organization and bring them to GE. Sometimes outside experts may actually be consulting firms, as described by Jim Bennett, who was the chairman of retail banking at Key Corp. and is now president and CEO of EmployOn:

> I always reach for the best people I can. When you are solving a tough business problem, you need access to the best, whether they are inside or outside. I look for first-class resources and have used McKinsey, Deloitte, and others. This can be kind of a foreign notion to consultant-averse or outsider-averse companies.

In searching for the best outside advice, we recommend that you seek out true experts who come with multiple recommendations, carefully scope their involvement opportunities, and stay engaged in their activities. The last piece is particularly important to ensure that you take advantage of the knowledge available and the new knowledge created.

Control the quality of your input: garbage in, garbage out. "Garbage in, garbage out" is an old saying among computer programmers. One of the biggest challenges in developing meaningful KM codification systems is ensuring accurate and timely data availability. During the mid-1990s, many companies attempted to set up sophisticated KM systems with databases, repositories, and expert listings. Many became dismayed when the systems failed to generate value for organizations because the information in the systems was inaccurate or outdated, as described earlier by Bill Ross at GE.

Make sure that those without firsthand knowledge of the subject matter can interpret the inputs to your KM system. Also, make sure that any document can be retrieved via the relevant keywords or other search methodology. Remember, without the proper incentives and dedicated resources, KM systems become "garbage."

IMPLEMENTATION GUIDANCE

KM at McKinsey goes well beyond advanced databases and codification strategies; so should you. The culture at McKinsey revolves around knowledge sharing. For example, there is an unwritten rule in the Firm that every employee returns a phone call from another McKinsey-ite within 24 hours. Both of us learned the value of this as early in a project we contacted experts who were able to steer us in the right direction and prevent days of excess search efforts.

Knowledge transfer through discussion is another key part of KM at McKinsey. The Firm provides incentives for knowledge sharing. For example, performance evaluations include an assessment of how well a consultant supports and develops others. The Firm holds regular "Practice Olympics,"* where ad hoc teams of consultants at all levels work together to summarize learnings on a particular business topic, normally an area in which they recently completed work. The Firm invests quite a bit of money into making this a special event, with prizes, newsletters, time off for competition, and fully funded trips to exotic locations for the competitions. Teams compete at a local level and earn their way up to such places as Australia or Hawaii, based on the merit of their ideas and their contribution to the Firm's knowledge.

When establishing your KM culture, the entire organization must participate; partial efforts just don't cut it. This means that there must be support from the top and constant reinforcement. This may be easier for smaller companies but is just as important for such companies as Accenture (formerly Andersen Consulting), as described by Jeff Sakaguchi, a partner:

> I've always been impressed with the responsiveness of the partnership here. I find folks responding even more quickly than at McKinsey. The key is that the responsiveness must come across the board and at a consistently high rate. It is analogous to the FedEx situation in that 90 percent on time isn't worth it, but 98 percent is a positive breakthrough.

This level of responsiveness might be a tough goal to achieve, but it generates results that are worth the effort.

---

*"Practice" at the Firm refers to the various industry and functional groups in which consultants can participate. Industry groups include Banking, Energy, and Media; functional groups include Information Systems, Logistics, and Corporate Finance, among others.

EXERCISES

- Perform a KM audit. Using the KM schematic shown in Figure 3-3 (page 77), analyze your firm's performance in: culture, infrastructure, and technology. For example, is there a strong KM culture that is well understood, supported by top management, with incentives for use and active interaction of all employees? After assessing your performance on a scale of 1 to 5 (worst to best) in each area, try to identify opportunities for improvement.
- Write a memo to the key KM person in your organization. The starting point in this exercise is to identify the person with responsibility for KM. This may be an actual chief knowledge officer (CKO), the CEO, the IT director, or the human resources director. Once you have identified the person, draft a brief memo requesting information related to the questions mentioned in the previous exercise. Hold off on your assessment and recommendation until you get a response. Every organization has a need for KM, and everyone in the organization should understand it, but these things take time (and sensitivity in some cases).

CONCLUSION

So there you have it—the wild, wonderful world of data gathering. Our goal in this chapter is to help you use data gathering to add value. In many organizations, too much energy is spent gathering the wrong data, and too many decisions are made without adequate data support. In this chapter, we hope you learned how to design more effective data-gathering efforts and picked up some specific tools that will help you. Happy hunting.

4

INTERPRETING THE RESULTS

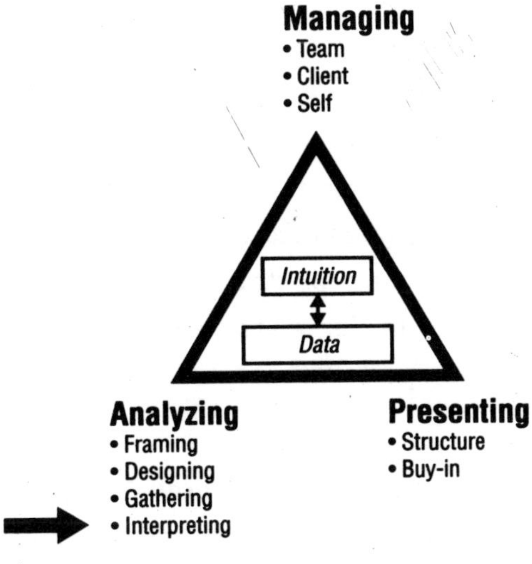

In the first three chapters of this book, we took you from the generation of an initial hypothesis, through the design of an analysis plan, up to the gathering of data upon which to apply that analysis. In many ways, these are the easy parts of the McKinsey problem-solving process. Now comes the hard part: figuring out what it all means.

A hypothesis, after all, must still be proved or disproved, and data on their own are mute. It is up to you and your team to use those facts to generate insights that will add value to your organization. All the multimegabyte spreadsheets and three-dimensional animated pie charts in the world don't mean anything unless someone can figure out the actions implied by these analyses and their value to the organization. McKinsey's consultants realize that clients don't, at the end of the day, pay for fancy documents and pretty slide shows. They pay for advice that will add value to their businesses; this is the end product of the consulting process and, by extension, of business problem solving in general. As Jeff Sakaguchi, who has moved from McKinsey to rival consulting firm Accenture, recalls:

> It's not just about research and analysis; it's research, analysis, and insight development. McKinsey focused on generating insights, specifically insights that had great client impact. I take pride, since I've joined Accenture, in having restructured some of our training for strategy consultants to drive home that mentality in our teams and really make it an explicit part of our performance evaluation process for consultants.

In this chapter, we will show you how McKinsey-ites draw conclusions from their analyses and turn them into useful recommendations for their clients, and how you can do the same in your company. We divide analysis interpretation into two parts. First comes the process of *understanding the data*: piecing together (in your own mind or within the confines of your team) the story the data are telling you and the steps you should take based on that story. Second comes assembling your findings into an externally directed *end product*: a course of action for your organization or client.

UNDERSTANDING THE DATA

After you've run all the numbers and conducted all the interviews, you will have a huge pile of facts to sift through. Your job is to sort the wheat from the chaff, to separate the irrelevant factoids from the data that actually prove or disprove your hypothesis, and then to piece together the story those data tell. This requires not just the ability to understand the meaning of the individual analyses, but the imagination to put the disparate facts together into a coherent narrative. This is not always easy, as one of our more blunt-spoken alumni said: "It's a whole lot easier to gather and package data than it is to think."

The actual techniques you would use to analyze your data will vary depending on the individual analyses you are doing, the company you work for, and the business in which you operate. In this section, rather than demonstrate any particular analysis, we will show you how to take the results of whichever analyses you choose and assemble them into something that will allow you to make a very important decision.

Yogi Berra famously remarked, "If you come to a fork in the road, take it." At this point in the problem-solving process, you've reached a fork in the road; the results of your analyses can take you in one of two directions. If your analysis proves your hypothesis, then you need to move on to the next section of this chapter and figure out what course of action the data imply. If the data disprove your hypothesis, then you need to revisit and restructure your initial hypothesis to fit the data. This may or may not require additional analysis as well. We, with the help of our alumni, will show you how to choose which fork to take.

THE McKINSEY WAY

McKinsey-ites use the following principles in their daily struggles with data analysis.

80/20. The 80/20 rule is one of the great truths of business. It is a rule of thumb that says 80 percent of an effect under study will be generated by 20 percent of the examples analyzed. This rule dates back to the economist Vilfredo Pareto. While researching economic conditions in his native Italy, Pareto determined that 20 percent of the population owned 80 percent of the land. Subsequently, while working in his garden, he discovered that about 80 percent of his peas came from just 20 percent of his plants. Based on these and other observations, he determined that for any series of elements under study, a small fraction of the number of elements usually accounts for a large fraction of the effect. Over time, Pareto's observation became generalized as the 80/20 rule.

Although the 80/20 rule has been around a lot longer than McKinsey, McKinsey consultants live and die by it. If you look at the numbers that drive your organization, almost invariably, you will find instances of 80/20. For instance, you may determine that 80 percent of your sales comes from 20 percent of your clients, 20 percent of your sales staff generate 80 percent of your profits, 80 percent of your time is spent on 20 percent of your job.

The 80/20 rule is all about data. When you're doing a data-intensive analysis on your computer, play around with the numbers a bit. Sort them in various ways. Whenever you see 80/20 in action, you should look for the opportunities it implies. If 80 percent of your sales come from 20 percent of your sales force, then what is that 20 percent doing right, and how can the 80 percent be brought up to speed? Do you really need the other 80 percent at all? As you can see, a little bit of 80/20 can go a long way.

Make a chart every day. At the end of each day, ask yourself, "What are the three most important things I learned today?" Take half an hour before you leave your desk to put it down on paper—nothing fancy, just a hastily sketched chart or a few bullet points will do. This exercise will help you push your thinking. Whether you use that chart or not, once you've drawn it, you won't forget it. Otherwise, the brilliant insight you had this morning might get lost by the time you lock up your desk tonight.

Don't make the facts fit your solution. You and your team may have formulated a brilliant hypothesis, but when it comes time to prove or disprove it, be prepared for the facts and analyses to prove you wrong. If the facts don't fit your hypothesis, then it is your hypothesis that must change, not the facts.

LESSONS LEARNED AND IMPLEMENTATION ILLUSTRATIONS

When interpreting your analyses, you have two parallel goals: you want to be quick, and you want to be right. Obviously, these two goals are sometimes in conflict. It's usually worth taking an extra day if that will make the difference between getting the right answer and the wrong one. However, as we discussed in Chapter 2, there's probably little point in spending an extra week to go from three decimal places of accuracy to four.

The results of our survey of McKinsey alumni led us to draw the following conclusions about data interpretation:

- Always ask, "What's the so what?"
- Perform sanity checks.
- Remember that there are limits to analysis.

Always ask, "What's the so what?" When you put together your analysis plan (as we discussed in Chapter 2), you were supposed to eliminate any analyses, no matter how clever or interesting, that didn't get you a step closer to proving or disproving your original hypothesis. No matter how good your work plan, however, it is almost inevitable that you will have to go through another filtering process once you've gathered the data, crunched the numbers, and interpreted the interviews. Some of your results will turn out to be dead ends: interesting facts, neat charts, but nothing that helps you get closer to a solution. It's your job to weed out these irrelevancies.

At McKinsey, the shorthand for this process was for someone on the team, usually the EM, to ask, "What's the so what?" for a particular analysis. What does it tell us, and how is that useful? What recommendation does it lead to? Consultants aren't in the business of drawing pretty pictures, and that's not what their clients pay them lots of money to do. As Jeff Sakaguchi learned at McKinsey and continues to preach at Accenture:

> Consulting isn't about analysis; it's about insights. If you can't draw an insight from what you've just done, then it's a waste of time. Crunching numbers for the sake of crunching numbers, or doing bar charts for the sake of doing bar charts, doesn't help unless it brings to life some insight, some key finding, that will make your team and your client say, "Hmm, interesting."

A consultant must take the disparate messages of his analyses and synthesize them into insights that will solve his client's problem. That happens best when every analysis meets the test of "So what?"

Perform sanity checks. Obviously, one wants to be as accurate as possible, but in a team situation you, as team leader, probably don't have time to perform a detailed check on every analysis your team produces. Whenever someone presents you with a new recommendation or insight, however, you can do a quick sanity check to ensure that the answer at least sounds plausible. Like the QDT we presented in Chapter 1, a sanity check lets you swiftly ascertain whether a particular analysis is at least within the bounds of probability. A sanity check consists of a few pointed questions, the answers to which will show whether a recommendation is feasible and whether it will have a noticeable impact on the organization.

The exact question will vary with every situation, but here are some examples, courtesy of our alumni:

> I can use an off-the-shelf, easy-to-use program like MS Access to disprove a stupid theory very fast. For example, an employee had a hypothesis that we should request that merchandise be returned to the warehouse based on minimum rather than maximum inventory levels. I was able to test that idea in two minutes to determine that it would result in only $4,000 of a projected return of $400,000. Not worth the loss of a week to reprint and send procedures for the stores to follow.
>
> —Bob Buchsbaum, CEO, Dick Blick Holdings

→ → →

> I like to use scenario analysis. I'll ask, "What would it take to have this matter?" For example, how many leads would we have to generate off the website for it to show up as anything more than a rounding error? If the answer is 10 gazillion, well, I doubt we'll get that many. If the answer is 50, then I'll say, "Oh, OK." If the assumptions behind the analysis don't make sense, then you can move on to the next idea.
>
> —Dan Veto, Senior Vice President, Conseco

→ → →

> I actually had an analyst run lots of numbers from many different sources and then come to me and say, "Well, here's the answer." I took one look at the numbers and said that can't possibly be right, because if it were, the world would look a whole lot different. So, when you're analyzing the data, just be sure that you're stepping back from it and doing a high-level sanity check.
>
> —Bill Ross, General Electric

→ → →

> I always ask, "How far off would our current answer need to be before we change our conclusion?" I push very hard on testing assumptions by making sure the drivers of those assumptions are very clearly identified. I then focus the analysis on these drivers. This has fundamentally improved our acquisition strategy; the results of our recent acquisitions speak for themselves.
>
> —Ron O'Hanley, President, Mellon Institutional Asset Management

Although there's no one best way to do a sanity check, asking a few pointed questions about your analyses before you put together your big presentation can save you a lot of trouble.

Remember that there are limits to analysis. Analysis plays a vital role in the McKinsey problem-solving process, but when all is said and done, it can take you only so far. You have to draw inferences from the analyses; they won't speak for themselves. You've reached the point in our consulting model where intuition takes the lead from data. You've come to Mr. Berra's fork in the road, and you have to take it.

That analysis has its limitations is no reason to dispense with it, however. Beware what one of our alumni described as the "ready, fire, aim mentality." Even if you are a skilled decision maker with reliable intuition, good analysis helps support and communicate your solution throughout your organization, as Bill Ross describes:

> In many cases, executives, being smart business leaders, have already gone through the problem-solving process internally without laying it out for others to see. If you go through their thinking with them, however, you'll often find they've missed an option. More importantly, *they* may be ready to move quickly, but they still have to pull their whole organization along with them. Without having documented and communicated some of their thought process, there's no way that they can bring their organization along except by brute force. We know that doesn't work for very long, because if you keep at it, then people just wait for you to tell them where to go next.

While some like to think of intuition and data as polar opposites, yin and yang, they actually work together. And like yin and yang, each needs the other to thrive. Data without intuition are merely raw information, and intuition without data is just guesswork. Put the two together, however, and you have the basis for sound decision making.

IMPLEMENTATION GUIDANCE

At this stage in the problem-solving process, you need to figure out what the facts are telling you. The economist John Maynard Keynes, when berated by a critic for contradicting one of his earlier assertions, famously said, "When the facts change, I change my mind. What do you do, sir?" Transferring this to the context of the McKinsey problem-solving process, when the facts contradict your hypothesis, you should change your hypothesis, not suppress the facts. We can't stress this too much. When you've spent a lot of time and effort coming up with what you consider a brilliant hypothesis, it's easy to become wedded to it, refusing to believe that you just might be wrong.

McKinsey offered several lessons on this topic: "Don't make the facts fit your solution"; "Be prepared to kill your babies" (offered in the context of brainstorming, but it holds just as much for data analysis); and "Just say, 'I don't know.'" What was true at the Firm holds just as true outside of it. There is an iterative loop that runs from hypothesis to analysis design to research to interpretation and then, if necessary, back to hypothesis. Only after you have definitively proved your final, modified hypothesis are you ready to put together the end product—the advice that you will give to your client.

When we asked our McKinsey alumni what tools they use to help them make sense of the data, they almost all mentioned the 80/20 rule. As we discussed earlier in this chapter, 80/20 manifests itself in a variety of ways. To offer a few more examples, 20 percent of the population in the United States pays 80 percent of the income tax. Of the students in a classroom, 20 percent occupy 80 percent of a teacher's time. You might choose 80 percent of the outfits you wear from 20 percent of your wardrobe. We could go on and on. The 80/20 rule is not always strictly true; in one case, the true ratio may be 75/25, in another 90/10. Furthermore, it is not universally applicable, but it occurs so frequently as to make it a useful predictive tool.

At McKinsey, the 80/20 is primarily about data, and that's certainly true as far as it goes. Applying the 80/20 rule to numerical data can lead to all sorts of insights that pass the "So what?" test. Returning to the earlier example, if you learn that 20 percent of your sales staff account for 80 percent of your sales, you should immediately ask why that is and what can be done to bring the rest of the sales team up to the level of the top performers. Note that the 80/20 rule doesn't necessarily lead directly to insight. Rather, it prompts you to ask new questions and possibly perform new analyses that will help you put the story together.

Furthermore, 80/20 can go beyond data. It's also a useful tool for figuring out what story to tell. After all, 80 percent of your recommendations will come from 20 percent of your analyses. In a word, prioritize. Consider which of your recommendations will yield the most value for your client, and focus on them. Remember that an organization can only do so much at one time. Concentrate on the big wins first.

EXERCISES

- Think of the last analysis project you worked on or were presented with. Did each exhibit in the presentation you gave or saw meet the "So what?" test? Go through the presentation documents and write down the "so what" for at least 10 exhibits.
- Perform an 80/20 analysis of your job. On what do you spend most of your time? Which of your activities produce the most benefit for your organization? (Be honest!) Which produce the most benefit for you? Can you think of ways to spend more time on the things that produce the most benefit and less time on the activities that produce the least?
- Perform an 80/20 analysis of your company. Can you find instances of 80/20 in your business unit or department?

Which of your products or services produce most of your profit? Which consume most of your expenses? Can you find other instances of 80/20?

GENERATING THE END PRODUCT

Up to now, we've been dealing exclusively with the internal components of the problem-solving process. Forming your hypothesis, planning your work, doing your research, and interpreting your results—these all happen within the confines of your own office or team room. Theoretically, if you could get all your data without interviewing, you could complete all those steps without leaving your office, assuming you have a decent Internet connection (access to plumbing facilities might be convenient, too).

Now, however, we've reached the nexus between you (or your team) and your client: the end product. By "end product," we don't mean the collection of charts, slides, computer images, and other props that you use to communicate your solution to your audience; that will come in Chapter 5, "Presenting Your Ideas." End product, for our purposes, means the actual message that you will communicate. This is a subtle distinction but a meaningful one. Your interpretation of the data leads to a story, that is, what you think the data means. You select those portions of the story that you believe your audience needs to know in order to understand your conclusion, along with the supporting evidence, and you put them together into your end product. Finally, you'll communicate that end product via one or more presentation media. The message and the medium are separate entities, whatever Marshall McLuhan may have said.*

*McLuhan, the celebrated Canadian communications commentator, is best remembered for writing, "The medium is the message."

In this section, we show you how to move from the story to the solution.

THE McKINSEY WAY

McKinsey has one principle relevent to this section: you must make sure the solution fits your client.

Make sure the solution fits your client. Management, like politics, is the art of the possible. The most brilliant solution, backed up by libraries of data and promising billions in extra profits, is useless if your client or business can't implement it. Know your client. Know the business's strengths, weaknesses, and capabilities—what management can and cannot do. Tailor your solutions with these factors in mind.

LESSONS LEARNED AND IMPLEMENTATION ILLUSTRATIONS

When McKinsey consultants leave the Firm and join other organizations, they often find that the challenge of generating an end product as an insider is, if anything, greater than it was as an outside consultant. The lessons from our McKinsey alumni reflect this, as they expand on the idea of fitting your solution to your client:

- See through your client's eyes.
- Respect the limits of your client's abilities.

See through your client's eyes. When McKinsey consultants talk about their organization, whether recruiting new consultants or undergoing a "beauty parade" for a potential client, eventually someone will utter the term *CEO focus* (or sometimes *top management focus*). CEO focus is the external counterpart to finding the key drivers: it's *your* view of what the five or six priorities of the organization ought to be. This is the first step toward seeing through your client's eyes because it forces you to concentrate on the client's foremost needs, even if some of them don't immediately affect what you're doing. Accenture's Jeff Sakaguchi explains:

> Even though we may not even be working on that specific area, keeping those things in mind certainly gives us a better sensitivity for the types of things that the client is or should be wrestling with. I've found many times that if I have a good picture of what the CEO agenda should be—even if it may not be what that current CEO is working on—sooner or later they come around to my way of thinking.

Depending on your position and power within your organization and on your corporate culture, you may have to rely on someone else's conception of the CEO focus (perhaps, even, your CEO's). Nevertheless, the CEO focus should be your touchstone as you put together your recommendation.

As your next step, ask how your decisions will add value to your client or organization. For each action that you recommend, how large will the payoff be? Is it large enough to justify the required commitment of time, energy, and resources? How does it compare to the other recommendations you make? If it is significantly smaller in terms of potential result, other, larger projects should come first. As chair of retail banking at Key Corp., Jim Bennett had to make decisions like this every day:

> For me, the metric has to be, "Is this really going to make a difference?" At Key, as in most companies, decisions are typically input-oriented rather than performance- and output-oriented. We tried to change that paradigm by going public with performance commitments—"We're going to grow our earnings by *X*"—which put us on the hook to come up with projects that would meet that goal. This focus on funda-

> mental and lasting differences in performance forces us to take an aggressive 80/20 view of any potential project. We have to ask, "If we commit these resources for something approaching this predicted return, what difference is it going to make to hitting our performance objective?"
>
> For example, my staff brought me a data warehouse project which required an investment of $8 million for a wonderful internal rate of return and payback in two or three years. I said, "Look, guys, if we can't get at least 10 times the impact for this expenditure, I'm not taking this to the board, so go back and find some way that we're going to generate a return of at least 10 times whatever it is we spend." Everything is judged on its ability to help us meet our performance challenge.

Sometimes you can get caught up in the elegance and cleverness of your analysis, or even the sheer effort you put into it. Don't let it cloud your judgment. With apologies to Jack Kennedy, "Ask not what your analysis means to you; ask what it can mean to your client."

Respect the limits of your client's abilities. The most brilliant strategy in the world won't help you if your organization can't implement it. This holds not just for business, it's true in any realm that calls for strategy. If your football team doesn't have a strong offensive line, there's no point trying to run the ball up the middle. In World War II, the Germans couldn't sustain a two-front war. In U.S. politics, you don't embark on a legislative campaign if you can't muster a majority in Congress (as McKinsey alumna Sylvia Mathews learned from her experience at the Office of Management and Budget).

When putting together your end product, therefore, keep in mind whether the recommendations you are making are actionable for the client. Does your client have the skills, systems, structures, and staff to do what is required? Will outside forces—competitors, suppliers, customers, regulators—take actions that will nullify the effects of your strategy? If you've planned your analysis correctly in the first place, you should be able to answer these questions before you make your recommendation.

At a level below that of grand strategy, you should also consider whether your analysis and recommendations will be understandable to the organization as a whole. We will examine this issue with regard to the actual packaging of your message in Chapter 5, but your analysis itself, in most instances, should be understandable to outsiders. The main reason is that by making your analysis accessible to those who have to decide on and implement it, you will make it easier for them to support it. Paul Kenny discovered that principle at GlaxoSmithKline:

> A lot of the models that we use for analyzing diseases are overly complex: they are multimegabyte, hundreds of pages, or interlocking Excel spreadsheets. You wouldn't believe some of the ones I've inherited. I've had a two-megabyte model linking with another model linking with another model, and you'd look at one of these things and have no idea how to work your way through it. One of the principles that I learned at McKinsey that I always apply when building any sort of model is to keep it simple, keep it focused, keep it brief. As a result, I typically do one-page models, and I try to keep them simple and transparent, so that the audience can see the mechanics rather than getting lost in the detail. You don't lose much by leaving out that detail either; on the contrary, you can focus on the key drivers and see what is happening.

We'll discuss simplicity more fully in Chapter 5. For now, we'll just say that even if the particular analysis you are doing necessitates gigabyte-sized models and complex mathematics, try to simplify the results of that analysis to a level that an educated outsider can understand.

IMPLEMENTATION GUIDANCE

At the beginning of this section, we stated that once you have all the facts (the results of all your analyses), your job is to piece together a story from some, but not all, of those facts. You may wonder why you shouldn't tell the whole story and use everything you have. To tell you why, we'd like to use a nonbusiness analogy that may be familiar: the story of King Arthur and his knights of the Round Table.

Although King Arthur and his knights may have been completely or mostly legendary, "facts" about them abound. If you dig around, you will turn up sources dating back to the last millennium—that is, A.D. 1000—and beyond from Wales, England, France, Germany, Italy, and no doubt from other places. Authors and storytellers have pieced these sources together in many different ways over the centuries, resulting in works as diverse as Malory's *Le Morte d'Arthur*, T. H. White's *The Once and Future King*, the musical *Camelot*, and movie versions ranging from John Boorman's graphic *Excalibur* to Disney's *Sword in the Stone* (not to mention the Mr. Magoo version). Yet these very different end products all stem from the same set of "facts" (and if you want to see just how different they are, watch *Excalibur* followed by *Monty Python and the Holy Grail*).

Each of these storytellers has a different story to tell and a different audience to tell it to, yet at some level, they are the same story. When you have to put your facts into a coherent story for your client, you have the same goal as an author writing her own version of the story of Arthur: making your audience understand your message. What separates you from a writer of fiction or a movie director is your responsibility to be intellectually honest. The author can depict her Arthur however she wants to make her point or press her agenda. As a result, audiences have seen Arthur as a blood-soaked conqueror (*Excalibur*), a noble but doomed king (*Le Morte d'Arthur*), an innocent boy (*The Sword in the Stone*), and a very silly man who says "Ni" to old ladies (*Monty Python and the Holy Grail*). You, as a consultant or employee, don't have that freedom:* you have to produce recommendations that will add the most value to your client.

Remember that the goal of the problem-solving process—your goal—is not simply to come up with a brilliant idea. If you ask a McKinsey consultant what it is that the Firm does, one of the most common answers you will receive is, "We help our clients make change happen." They won't say, "We come up with brilliant ideas for our clients." They realize that the best idea or the cleverest strategy is worth precisely nothing if the client doesn't buy into it and implement it. To secure that buy-in, you have to put together a compelling narrative, and that entails leaving out facts that don't advance your story.

Please note, this does not mean you should ignore evidence that contradicts your hypothesis. Quite the contrary; by this time, you should already have adjusted your hypothesis to the facts. It does mean that you should not throw every fact that you have into your story just because you can. If you do so, you will lose your audience in irrelevant detail, and this will get in the way of telling your story.

*Unfortunately, that hasn't stopped people from producing business plans straight out of Monty Python.

EXERCISES

- Get a copy of an annual report—preferably from your own company. Based on the information in the annual report, decide whether the company's stock is a good investment. Give five reasons why, in order of their importance.
- Thinking about your own organization, what are the five or six issues on which the CEO should focus? How does your job affect these issues, and what could you do to have more impact?
- Make a list of the strengths and limitations of your organization. Put them into a MECE categorization. Think about whether your organization's recent projects have played to those strengths and limitations. How could future projects be better suited to them?

CONCLUSION

As we've shown, interpreting the data has two components. Internally, you piece together the facts into a coherent picture that leads you to a recommendation. Externally, you assemble certain facts into an end product that you will use to communicate your recommendation to your client. At this point, you have seen the problem-solving process from start to finish. We believe that if you follow the recommendations we have made so far, you will be able to improve the quality and speed of decision making in your organization. Your work doesn't end there, however. Now, you have to communicate your ideas to the critical decision makers in your organization, and possibly to the organization as a whole. For that, you will need the presentation strategies in the next chapter.

5

PRESENTING YOUR IDEAS

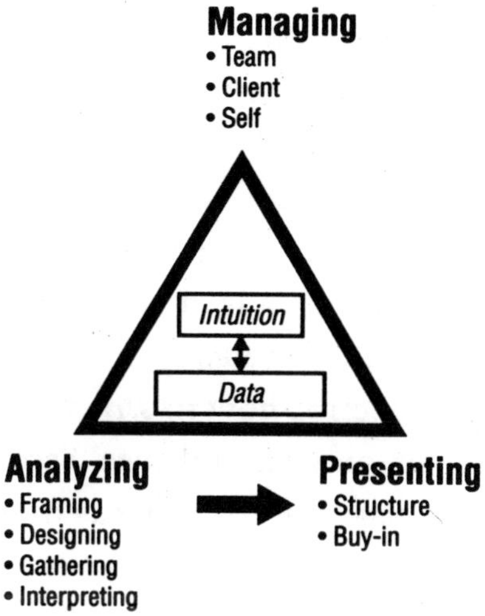

We've now reached the final stage in the McKinsey problem-solving process: presenting your ideas. All the hypothesizing, all the work planning, all the research, and all the analysis have led up to this point, but if you don't get this part right, all your efforts will have been a waste of time. If you piled up all the good business ideas that withered on the vine for want of an effective presentation, you'd top the Empire State Building. In this chapter, we will show you how to keep your ideas out of that pile.

If there is a stereotype of McKinsey in the minds of businesspeople, it is the image of a formal presentation conducted by men in dark suits and white shirts around the boardroom table. This image grows increasingly out of date in today's business environment; the Firm does far fewer formal presentations than it did 10 years ago. However, the men and women of McKinsey continue to rely on presentations in one form or another to convey ideas to the Firm's clients. To this end, McKinsey has developed a highly effective set of presentation and communication skills for its consultants to use.

In the experience of our McKinsey alumni, these skills, more than any others they learned at the Firm, translate almost unaltered to other organizations. With them, McKinsey alumni get their ideas across—and get them accepted. McKinsey-style presentations work so well that one alumnus even called them an unfair advantage. You can have that advantage, too.

In this chapter, we examine two aspects of presentation à la McKinsey. First, we describe how to *structure* your presentation to maximize its impact on your audience. Second, we detail techniques for generating *buy-in* for your ideas from your audience.

STRUCTURE

McKinsey spends a lot of time training its consultants to structure their presentations, and they take this training seriously—even if it often takes place in exotic locations near good golf courses. When it comes to presentation, McKinsey consultants learn that a presentation must convey ideas to the audience in the clearest, most convincing way possible. To ensure that your presentation meets this goal, you need to give it a structure that the audience can easily grasp and follow.

In this section we will show you how to structure your presentations for maximum effect. You'll see how to arrange your ideas into a logical flow that your audience can absorb and how to use charts to get your message across.

THE McKINSEY WAY

When it comes to presentation structure, McKinsey emphasizes organization and simplicity.

Be structured. For your presentation to succeed, it must take the audience down the path of your logic in clear, easy-to-follow steps. Your presentation is a manifestation of your thought process. If your thinking is clear and logical, your presentation should be, too. Conversely, if your thinking is muddled, you will have a hard time putting your ideas into a sound structure.

The elevator test. Sometimes you don't have much time to make your case. Know your solution (or your product or business) so thoroughly that you can explain it clearly and precisely to your client in the course of a 30-second elevator ride. If you can pass this "elevator test," then you understand what you're doing well enough to sell your solution.

Keep it simple—one message per chart. The more complex a chart becomes, the less effective it is at conveying information. The meaning of a chart should be immediately obvious to the reader, so use whatever tools you need to bring it out. If you want to use the same chart to make multiple points, redraw it for each point and highlight the relevant information in each chart.

Use charts as a means of getting your message across, not as an art project. McKinsey has always erred on the side of conservatism when it comes to graphics. You won't see a lot of color or 3-D graphics in a McKinsey presentation—unless such features are necessary to communicate the point of the chart.

LESSONS LEARNED AND IMPLEMENTATION ILLUSTRATIONS

Of all the skill sets that apply to the McKinsey problem-solving process, structuring presentations requires the least adaptation to the outside world. Effective communication is effective communication pretty much anywhere, and the Firm's methods are extremely effective. As venture capitalist Ciara Burnham of Evercore Partners notes:

> McKinsey provides outstanding training in written communications. The McKinsey problem-solving process forces one to be logical and clear about each issue and its implications. It also serves as a useful check of the thoroughness of one's analysis: when I am having trouble writing a presentation, it is usually because my logic and analysis are not completely clear.

Given how powerful these techniques are, it didn't surprise us that comments from our alumni centered on one main lesson regarding presentation structure: support your ideas with a solid structure.

Support your ideas with a solid structure. Stripped to its essence, presentation is selling. You and your team may appreciate the brilliance of your ideas and the quality of all the work you've done, but your client, your colleagues, or your organization may not. You have to convince them, and your presentation is your best tool for doing so. Make no mistake, presentation matters. That has been the experience of Bob Garda, formerly a director of McKinsey's Cleveland office, later CEO of a brand-name consumer goods manufacturer, and now a professor at the Fuqua School of Business: "I've put half-baked ideas into great presentations and seen them soar, and I've put great ideas into bad presentations and watched them die."

Unfortunately, in today's corporate world, a lot more ideas are dying than soaring, if the experiences of our McKinsey alumni are typical. The poor quality of presentations in their new organizations came as a shock to many of them. Here are a few typical impressions (with the names changed to protect the innocent):

> I look at the kind of presentations our senior managers give to each other and to our customers, and it's depressing. People don't know how to structure an argument. Their presentations are just stream of consciousness. This was the most startling change for me when I left McKinsey.
>
> —An alumnus in the health care industry

→ → →

> I'm always amazed at the poor quality of the presentations here. We tend to have words or outlines put on PowerPoint slides; people actually think that's a presentation. It's not. If all you have is bullet points with nothing to show graphically with a chart or schematic, then in my mind, you should put it in a memo that you send out before the meeting. We have a lot of meetings where we *read* outlines together. No charts for anything. It's like kindergarten.
>
> —An alumnus in financial services

→ → →

> I worked with a senior executive who always took hours to build to a point. The "so what" of his slides seemed to be

> "Here's a lot of data I know." The board would become visibly agitated during his presentations. It took me two years to break him of this habit.
>
> —An alumnus in the retail industry

It's no wonder they sound frustrated. A poor presentation can make a good idea tough for an audience to grasp. More often, though, a poorly designed presentation reflects a poorly thought-out idea. It's difficult to put incoherent thoughts into a coherent structure.

Conversely, a well-written presentation in service to a good idea can be a powerful instrument of change. Communicating a course of action throughout an organization acts as a catalyst. When Bob Garda became CEO of a brand-name consumer goods manufacturer, he had just such an experience:

> Most people don't feel comfortable structuring a coherent presentation that lays out a theme from which the subthemes emerge. When I arrived on the scene, the company lacked a clear vision for the future: what the organization was and what it wanted to be when it grew up. Vision was one of the first things that I felt we needed to address, and just the fact that I was able to put together a presentation around that theme—because I felt very comfortable laying out my ideas in a structured manner—had a tremendous impact.

This ability to present ideas in a flowing, logical structure lies behind the Firm's self-proclaimed ability to "make change happen." It's not just that McKinsey consultants come up with good ideas; it's that they can communicate the full impact of these ideas to their clients. This skill carries over extremely well into the outside world. As S. Neil Crocker, general manager of Pearson PLC's Virtual University Enterprises, remarks:

> Strong communications skills supported by strong logic wipe out most concerns. I have yet to be turned down by my CEO or board for anything that I really wanted. Presentation is the "killer skill" we take into the real world. It is almost an unfair advantage!

Fortunately, you don't have to work at McKinsey to learn how to put together an effective presentation. In fact, some McKinsey alumni have started teaching these skills in their own organizations. By the end of this section, we hope to have shown you enough about presentation structure that you can get the ball rolling in your organization, too.

IMPLEMENTATION GUIDANCE

A successful presentation bridges the gap between you—the presenter—and your audience. It lets them know what you know. You can make this process easy for your audience by giving your presentations a clear and logical structure. Fortunately, if you have been adhering to the principles of this book, then you already have a solid basis for such a structure: your initial hypothesis.

If you broke out your initial hypothesis into a MECE set of issues and subissues (and suitably modified them according to the results of your analysis), then you have a ready-made outline for your presentation. If you have a well-structured, MECE hypothesis, then you will have a well-structured, MECE presentation. Conversely, if you can't get your presentation to make sense, then you may want to rethink the logic of your hypothesis. Many of our McKinsey alumni found this a useful check on their thinking. Just put together the exhibits that prove your various points, and fit them into their proper place on the issue tree.

Figure 5-1. Acme Widgets Presentation: First Slide

As an example, let's go back to the Acme Widgets issue tree from Chapter 1 (see Figure 1-2, page 26). Your team came up with the initial hypothesis that Acme can lower the marginal cost of its thrum-mats by instituting a new, shorter curing process. Your analysis proves that the new process is cheaper, that Acme can implement the changes required to accommodate the new process, and that the new process will not diminish the quality of Acme's thrum-mats. Say so in your first slide (Figure 5-1). With that slide, you've established the structure of your presentation for your audience: they know where you're going and will have an easy time following you.

The rest of your presentation flows out of the first slide. Each of those major points under your initial hypothesis constitutes a section of your presentation. Each section will consist of the various levels of subissues under each of those major issues. For example, let's look at the second major issue, "Acme can implement the changes necessary to accommodate the new process," which we delved into in Chapter 1. The various subissues that arose from that discussion now form the major points for Section 2 of your presentation: we have the necessary facilities and the necessary skills within our organization (see Figure 5-2). You can repeat this process all the way down your issue tree, but you have the freedom not to go too deeply into detail, depending on your audience. At

Figure 5-2. Acme Widgets Presentation: Second Section Lead

We have the resources in place to implement the new process: • **We have facilities that can accommodate the new process.** • **Our people have the necessary skills to run the new process.**

whatever level of detail you stop, the logic of your presentation will still be clear.

You may have found one aspect of this structure unusual. We recommend starting with your conclusion—in the case of Acme Widgets, changing the thrum-mat production process. Many presentations take the opposite approach, going through all the data before finally springing the conclusion on the audience. While there are circumstances where this is warranted—you may really want to keep your listeners in suspense—it is very easy to lose your audience before you get to your conclusions, especially in data-intensive presentations. By starting with your conclusion, you prevent your audience from asking, "Where is she going with this?"

Having your conclusions or recommendations up front is sometimes known as inductive reasoning. Simply put, inductive reasoning takes the form, "We believe *X* because of reasons *A*, *B*, and *C*." This contrasts with deductive reasoning, which can run along the lines of, "*A* is true, *B* is true, and *C* is true; therefore, we believe *X*." Even in this simplest and most abstract example, it is obvious that inductive reasoning gets to the point a lot more quickly, takes less time to read, and packs a lot more punch. McKinsey prefers inductive reasoning in its communications for precisely these reasons, as Ron O'Hanley of Mellon attests:

> I always strive for a statement of conclusions up front in oral and written communications. This gets everybody on the

> same page, even if they disagree, and gives context to all of the supporting data and arguments. It also helps me be more efficient and effective in marshaling my arguments.

As an additional advantage, starting with your conclusions allows you to control how far you go into detail in your presentation. For example, suppose you are presenting in an interactive setting, say, to your boss in his office. You have three major points you want to communicate to him. Now, suppose that he already accepts your second point and doesn't need to be convinced with a lot of data. If you have organized your presentation deductively, then you will have to take him through all the supporting data for that point before you actually tell him your conclusion—which he already agreed with anyway. You've just wasted a lot of time for no particular gain. On the other hand, if you've taken the inductive approach, then your boss can simply give his agreement to your point at the outset. You can spend more time on the other points or get out of the meeting and back to work.

Putting your conclusions up front will also help you pass the elevator test. As we mentioned earlier in the chapter, you pass the elevator test when you can rattle off your conclusions in the space of an elevator ride. In fact, if you've followed the McKinsey method, then your first slide—with your recommendation and major points—is your answer to the elevator test. Imagine trying to pass the elevator test using a deductive outline—not easy, is it?

We strongly recommend that you take the elevator test before any presentation. Our McKinsey alumni gave us numerous examples of its usefulness in their careers. Here are a few testimonials:

> I'm in a post-start-up situation right now, with several former very senior executives from large companies. I find myself telling them, "Hey, we only have 20 minutes with Goldman Sachs, and only the first 2 count. Pretend you only

> have an elevator ride to get your point across to them. What are you going to say?" It's amazing how many successful people cannot simply focus on two or three key points and articulate them well.
>
> —Brad Farnsworth, GeoNetServices.com

> Throughout my career, the ability to say what I need to say in a short, sharp sound bite has paid off in many ways. As an author, I find it essential to getting great media coverage. The elevator test is simply about sound bites, and it is a great way to know if your product or idea is compelling enough to move a person to action. If I fail the elevator test, it not only says that my communication is not clear, but that the underlying issue is perhaps not compelling.
>
> —Deborah Knuckey, author of *The MsSpent Money Guide*

→ → →

> My board has attention spans similar to the elevator test. Without it, I would probably be dead!
>
> —An alumnus in academia

Perhaps the best summation of the value of the elevator test comes from Roger Boisvert of CTR Ventures: "In presenting businesses, my own especially, if I am not able to do the elevator test, I shouldn't be talking with anyone." If you can't articulate your thoughts clearly and concisely, then either you don't understand the material well enough and need to get better acquainted with it, or your structure is not clear and concise enough and needs to be reexamined.

As you might have guessed by now, we are zealous advocates of good presentation structure. However, even the best-designed, most logical set of recommendations imaginable still needs evidence to back it. Therefore, at this point, it's appropriate to look at the complement to your presentation's organizational structure: the exhibits you use to communicate your analyses.

These days, exhibits can be more than just charts on paper. They can be three-dimensional scale models, product samples, or Web pages, just to mention a few possibilities. Whatever form it takes, a good visual aid can be an incredibly effective communications tool. A picture is, after all, worth a thousand words. With charts, you can express in one image data and concepts that might take pages of text to describe. Not only that, but your audience often will absorb your point more readily when they can see it (and, in the case of physical models, touch it), rather than just hear it or read it.

Whether you are using good old black-and-white charts or rainbow-hued, three-dimensional computer animations with musical accompaniment, the lessons that McKinsey alumni learned still ring true. Most importantly, keep it simple. You're trying to communicate a set of recommendations, not show off an art project. While you may sometimes want to put together pretty pictures to impress your audience, the visual should not get in the way of the message. If you actually want it to do so, then you are not trying to communicate so much as obfuscate.

Each of your charts should have just one message for the audience to absorb, and the simpler, the better. That way, not only does your audience know what you're saying, you do, too. It's unlikely that you'll get confused in the middle of your presentation if your slides have only one clear message. When Sylvia Mathews was White House deputy chief of staff, preparing presentations for the President, she kept that principle foremost in her mind. Hey, if it works for the President of the United States . . .

One last, small thing about exhibits: if you are presenting data, always document your sources. That way, if someone asks you where you got your information, you'll be able to reply. In addition, if you dig out an old presentation a few years later, you'll know where to find the source.

As important as exhibits are, they're not enough; you still need a good structure in which to organize them. Otherwise, all you'll have is a collection of interesting facts with no overall theme. Remember, each exhibit is a message, and those messages have to fit into the logic of your structure, so your audience can understand your idea—which is, after all, the point of the exercise.

EXERCISES

- Search the editorial section of your favorite newspaper for an editorial that makes a specific recommendation. Write down the points the author makes and the evidence he uses to support them (e.g., we need more power plants because electricity use is rising 20 percent per year). Next, put those points into a logical structure as if you were going to use them for a presentation. Does this presentation get the message across? If not, why not?
- The next time you have to make a presentation, perform a dress rehearsal and videotape it. If possible, give yourself time to view the tape before the presentation. Watch the tape as if you were a member of the intended audience, knowing only the information that the audience might be expected to know, including any handouts you intend to give the audience. From that perspective, does your presentation make sense? Were you convinced? Consider what

steps you might take that would improve the impact of your presentation.

- Find a chart (possibly from a previous presentation) that, the first time you looked at it, took you a long time to understand. Redraw it in a way that makes the message readily understandable. If the original contains multiple messages, you may have to draw more than one chart. Now show your new chart(s) to someone who hasn't seen the original. Can that person understand your version? If not, why not?

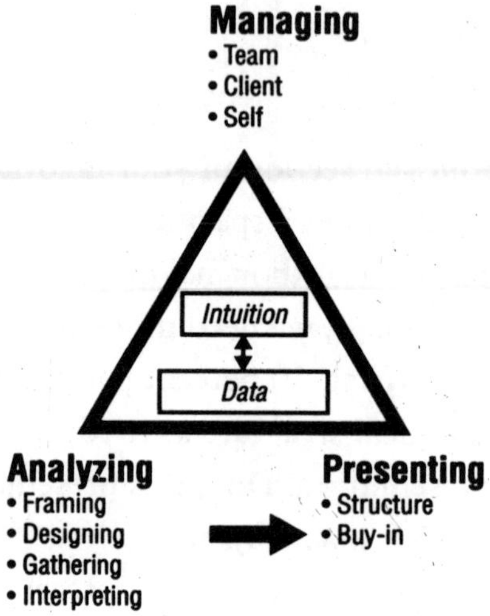

BUY-IN

A presentation is only a tool; it is not an end in itself. A great presentation, no matter how coherent its structure or how evocative its charts, is useless if the organization doesn't accept and act upon its recommendations. The shelves of Fortune 500 companies are stacked with presentation documents that never got out of the boardroom.

If your idea is to avoid a similar fate, you need to practice the gentle art of generating buy-in: taking the steps necessary to maximize the chance that your audience will accept your recommendations. These steps involve bridging the information and trust gaps between you. The information gap exists because you know more about your findings than your audience does. Depending on the relationship between you and your audience, the trust gap (if it exists) could take any of several forms. Your audience may think that you are too inexperienced to comment on their business, or they may mistrust you because you are an outsider, are overeducated (or not educated enough), or for any of a number of other reasons.

In this section, we will describe two ways to bridge these gaps: prewiring and tailoring. Prewiring means taking your audience through your findings before you give your presentation. Tailoring means adapting your presentation to your audience, both before you give it and, if necessary, on the fly. Together, these techniques will boost your chances of making change happen in your organization.

THE McKINSEY WAY

On the subject of buy-in, McKinsey alumni have one principle inscribed on their hearts: prewire everything.

Prewire everything. A good business presentation should contain no shocking revelations for the audience. Walk the relevant decision makers in your organization through your findings before you gather them together for a dog and pony show. McKinsey-ites have a shorthand expression for sending out your recommendations to request comment from key decision makers before a presentation: *prewiring*. At McKinsey, consultants learn to prewire every presentation.

Doing so has several advantages. It keeps you from getting blindsided by major objections to your solution. It also helps you build a consensus in favor of your solution among those who have to approve or implement it. It gives you a chance to adapt your solution to the political realities of your organization. Finally, it acts as an additional reality check on your findings. These consequences will improve the likelihood that your solution will be approved and implemented.

LESSONS LEARNED AND IMPLEMENTATION ILLUSTRATIONS

Because they want to be effective in their organizations, McKinsey alumni work hard at getting buy-in. Practically everyone who talked to us or returned a questionnaire mentioned the value of this strategy. We boiled their experiences down to two lessons:

- Avoid surprises.
- Tailor your presentation to your audience.

Avoid surprises. In business, people don't like surprises. By surprises, we don't mean getting an extra day off or a bigger than expected bonus; we mean new information that forces decision makers to change their plans or alter their procedures. That's why risky investments like small stocks have higher expected returns than safe investments like government bonds. Prewiring reduces your potential for surprises. It also acts as a check on your solutions because those who review your recommendations may mention something that you missed in your research and just might change your results.

More importantly, discussing your results outside the context of a large meeting increases your chances of getting those decision makers to buy into your ideas. In the intimacy of a one-on-one meeting, you open up your thought process to them in a way that is difficult to do in more formal settings. You can find out their concerns and address them. If someone takes issue with a particular recommendation, you may be able to work out a compromise before the big meeting, thereby ensuring that she will be on your side when the time comes.

To illustrate just how useful prewiring can be, we present a story told to us by Naras Eechambadi, now founder and CEO of Quaero, Inc., but previously the head of knowledge-based marketing for investment bank First Union. Naras used prewiring to great effect when he joined First Union:

> When I left the Firm I went to First Union to head up a group called Knowledge-Based Marketing. At the time, it was a very small group, and we wanted to grow it very rapidly. I had to present a business case to John Georgius, the president of First Union, to get the funding to scale it up over a three-year period. Using the interviewing techniques that I had learned at McKinsey, I spent my first two months talking to people in different parts of the company to discover their attitudes toward and expectations of our group. It was a very useful exercise, just structuring the guides and making sure I heard everybody. It was also part of the selling process.

Naras's ability to listen resulted in multiple benefits:

> I discovered that our group meant different things to different people. Some people expected too much; some people didn't expect enough. I got a sense of where the political land

> mines were. Then, rather than just taking it to the president directly, I went to all the heads of First Union's business units and told them what I was going to tell them, and got their feedback. I got a lot of buy-in because of this.
>
> I structured my business case just like a McKinsey presentation. People were struck by how organized, how thoughtful, and how forceful it was. We had scheduled a two-hour meeting, we finished it up in an hour and a half, and I had my acceptance by the end of the first hour—and it was a substantial investment. I think I'm still famous at First Union for being the guy who got money from John Georgius on the first try. Nobody had ever done that before.

Even if you can't get full agreement beforehand, prewiring will help you make your case, as Paul Kenny found when he was involved in a "battle of the presentations" at GlaxoSmithKline:

> I was killing a controversial product, and I had to make a very clear case to terminate it to some very senior champions for this particular project. Fortunately, I had done the groundwork beforehand. There was still resistance, but at least I knew where it was coming from. The key people knew the conclusions already. Some of them agreed, some of them disagreed, but at least we knew where we stood. In my presentation, I managed to bring together the key issues and get my recommendation across.

In a situation such as Paul describes, prewiring is especially helpful, because it forestalls wrangling over the facts of each individual point. Your audience already knows where you are coming from and can debate your ideas, rather than your facts.

Contrast Naras's and Paul's successes with someone who didn't take the time to prewire. In this case, a McKinsey alumnus was on the receiving end of a presentation that was full of surprises:

> I was on a Board in which the CEO didn't keep us sufficiently involved and informed. Over a period of a year, I talked to him off-line a grand total of once; other directors had the same experience. He needed to build alliances with Board members to implement his vision for the company. He needed to call Board members and say, "Here's where I want to take the company. I'd like to have your support for this or that." He should have understood who the power brokers were and made sure they were informed. You don't call a Board meeting out of the blue on Thursday to figure out whether or not you're going to buy a company on Sunday. The Board's response was, "We went through that two months ago and said we didn't want to do it then. Now you're calling an emergency meeting and giving us four days' notice?" Not a very smart thing to do without first building support. We subsequently parted ways.

You can avoid a similar fate by prewiring whenever and wherever you can.

Tailor your presentation to your audience. Tailoring means adapting your presentation to your audience, whoever it may include. Even if your audience comes from your own organization, the people in it may not share your background or knowledge of the subject matter. They may respond better to some styles of presentation than others: formal versus informal, large presentations versus intimate discussions, text-based versus audiovisual, just to name a few. Some people want to go into the minutiae, while others just want to hear your top-line arguments. If your presentation is to succeed, you need to know your audience, its preferences, and its background. Dean Dorman of Silver Oak Partners sums up our alumni's wisdom on tailoring:

> "McKinsey-izing" your presentations, using lots of consulting jargon—in most organizations, that gets you nowhere.

> Everything has to be completely tailored for your audience. A good leader knows his audience and how to relate to it.

Sometimes tailoring can even mean adjusting the structure of your presentation. If you know your audience has, say, little patience for supporting detail, what is the point of spending time on it? Just move right to your conclusions. Here's an example of tailoring from Bill Ross at GE:

> I still structure my pitches like we did at McKinsey—with an up-front page, governing thoughts, and some discussion of the background of the problem. Typically, though, I move through them much more quickly. At GE, you don't want to spend too much time on that. You want to jump much more quickly to the resolution. That's fine—you just spend less time on the charts that take people through the background. It's my version of "tell 'em what you're going to tell 'em, tell 'em, and then tell 'em what you told 'em."

The structure remains; you just highlight different aspects of it for different audiences.

Tailoring means more than just knowing your audience's likes and dislikes, however. You should also learn their language—the thought processes they rely on and the jargon they use. This is precisely what Naras Eechambadi did in the example we discussed in the section on prewiring:

> The two months I spent listening to people in First Union worked out very well for me because I got to understand what kind of language people used within the company, what kinds of things they were looking for, and what kind of outcomes they wanted. For the purposes of my own thinking, I used a McKinsey approach to solving the problem. But

when presenting it to the company, I used terms that were familiar to them, and I used an approach that was familiar to them. I didn't use the consulting methodology—the consulting lingo, if you will—in my presentation; I used theirs. I'm sure that's one reason my presentation was so well received.

Bear in mind that not only do different organizations have different languages; even different parts of the same organization can have different languages. You would not want to give the same presentation to, say, your company's board of directors and the drivers of your delivery trucks. It's nothing to do with how much smarter one is than the other, but that each group has different expectations, different goals, and a different language. These differences require you to tailor your message to each group.

IMPLEMENTATION GUIDANCE

The earlier you can start the prewiring process, the better. By identifying and getting input from the relevant players early on, you allow them to put their own mark on your solution, which will make them more comfortable with it and give them a stake in the outcome. You also give those outside your team a chance to expose any errors you may have made or opportunities you may have missed, and you still have time to correct them.

When it comes to tailoring, however, sometimes you have to act on the fly. A good presentation structure will give you the flexibility to change your pitch depending on the audience's reaction. You should never be so locked in to your script that you can't deviate from it if the occasion demands. Here's an example, courtesy of Bob Garda. In this case, he was actually a McKinsey client while taking a sabbatical to act as the temporary CEO of a major metropolitan utility:

> One of the associates on the McKinsey team got an appointment with me to cover the team's analysis of one of our problems and their initial recommendation. This young woman came in, sat down, and gave me one of the best lessons I've ever had. She said, "Let me tell you what I think the problem is," and started into her presentation. I said, "I think I understand the problem; let me tell you why," and gave her my assessment in four or so points. She replied, "That's right. So I don't need to waste your time telling you what your problem is. Let's just turn the first 16 pages over, and we'll go right to the solution." I don't ever recall hearing a McKinsey consultant say that before. That was a wonderful lesson for me.

Being flexible and, more importantly, respectful of your audience will gain you a lot of points.

You should also be aware of the physical circumstances of your presentation and adjust accordingly. You can deliver the same message using very different styles according to the setting. For instance, if you are meeting with three or four executives around a conference table, you probably don't need to use an overhead projector; a laser-printed "deck" of your exhibits should work fine. Conversely, if you have 50 people in an auditorium, you need to use something that will allow you to reach the people in the nosebleed seats.

EXERCISES

- Determine who the critical decision makers are for the issues you are currently tackling. What are their agendas, strengths, weaknesses, likes, dislikes, etc.? You might want to write these thoughts down for future reference.

- Identify the differences between two or more groups that interact with you regularly; they can be within your organization or outside of it—as different as your board and the Little League team you coach. Take a presentation you've previously done, and tailor it to each of these audiences. Ensure that your major message comes across in each version.

CONCLUSION

For McKinsey, presentation is where the rubber meets the road. A well-structured presentation combined with assiduous efforts to gain the buy-in of the key decision makers helps boost the odds of McKinsey's recommendation being accepted. These tactics can do the same for you.

You've given your presentation and had your recommendations accepted, but that doesn't mean the end of the work. A great idea, once accepted, still has to be implemented by the organization if it's to have any impact. That, however, is a different process and, perhaps, a different book.

Leaving aside implementation, the presentation of the team's final recommendation marks the end of the typical McKinsey consulting engagement. New problems requiring McKinsey's input may arise with the client, but they will be the occasion for the start of a new engagement. Likewise, in this book, we will now move from the process of creating and delivering solutions for business problems to the techniques required to manage that process for the benefit of the client, the team, and yourself.

6

MANAGING YOUR TEAM

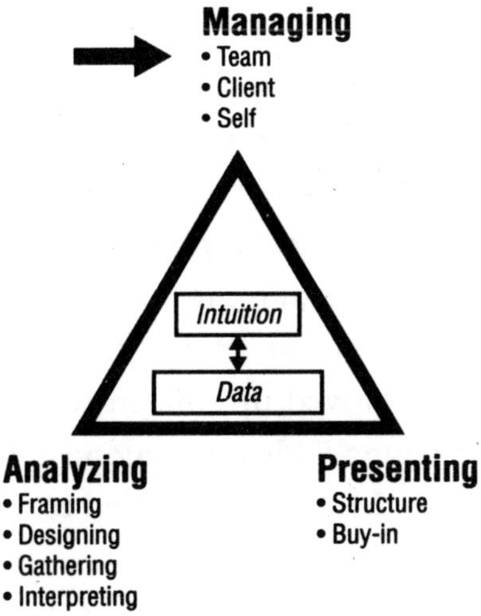

Over the past 20 years, the study of teams and leadership thereof has become one of the cornerstones of management theory. Most bookstores have at least one row (sometimes entire sections) dedicated to providing advice on how to create and lead a team. There is a reason for all of this advice: teams have become extremely common in organizations these days. There is a general belief that you can achieve more together than going at it alone. Not all teams are successful, however, and managing them can be difficult.

You would be hard-pressed to find an organization with more team-based activity than McKinsey. When it comes to managing those teams, depending upon whom you ask, the Firm is an excellent example of either what to do or what not to do. We will discuss both in this chapter. On the positive side, the Firm dedicates a lot of time and energy to training its team leaders with special training modules, conferences, and mentoring programs. Ciara Burnham of Evercore Partners elaborates: "One obvious lesson from McKinsey is that managing the team is a separate, distinct, and important task. This is not widely appreciated in other organizations."

Although McKinsey works very hard at building teams and team leaders, some say that the training comes too late in the game. One alumna, now with another strategy consulting firm, complains that some of the best team training came only at the higher ranks in McKinsey. "Managing the team was one of the areas in which I learned the least at McKinsey," he says. "There was some great material as you moved up, but in the early stages, it was mostly on-the-job training." He is not alone in his disappointment with some of the ways McKinsey handled teamwork and leadership training, as we will see in this chapter. Still, as evidenced by the Firm's great success over the past 75 years, it also knows how to do some things right.

We will cover four major elements of team management in this chapter: *team selection*, *internal communication*, *bonding activities*, and *individual development*.

SELECTION

You can't have a team without team members. That being the case, the first step to building a great team is selecting the right people.

In this section, we will discuss ways to make sure that you get the best possible people on your team. Sometimes, of course, the best person for your team might not be part of your organization. For that reason, this section will also look at ways to improve the efficiency and effectiveness of recruiting.

Perhaps you are in a situation where you have no control over the makeup of your team. In fact, based on our interviews with McKinsey alumni, that is more often the case than not in the world outside of McKinsey. Even so, at some future stage in your career, you might find yourself in a position to select your own team, especially if you follow the recommendations in the rest of this book.

THE McKINSEY WAY

Let's review McKinsey's approach to team selection and recruiting.

Getting the mix right. If you have the luxury of being able to pick your team, give some deliberate thought to your selections. McKinsey-ites make project assignment decisions based on the specific needs of the engagement. They carefully weigh raw intellect, experience, and interpersonal skills. Each aspect matters, but their relative importance can vary from project to project (and team to team).

If you have the opportunity, you should also try to meet any potential new members in person before you make a decision. Try to gain a sense of the chemistry among your team members. Don't just blindly accept others' word on the quality of a potential teammate. If at all possible, see for yourself.

Recruiting McKinsey-style. McKinsey wouldn't be McKinsey if it weren't very picky about whom it recruits. The Firm, according to its mission statement, strives to "attract, develop, excite, motivate and retain exceptional people," and it puts its money where its mouth is. Recruiting at McKinsey is led by the partners and supported by a number of full-time professionals and a huge budget.

McKinsey carries out its strategy by searching for the highest performers in the best business schools in the world and has, over time, expanded its sources to include the highest performers in other schools, disciplines, and industries.

The recruiting process at McKinsey involves numerous, intensive case study interviews. A candidate can expect to see at least eight different consultants during the interview process, each with a different case to solve. The Firm's goal is to take a deep look into each candidate's mind to assess his analytical and interpersonal abilities and decide whether the candidate would be a good fit. Overall, the best strategy for making it through the rigorous recruiting process at McKinsey is to have a strong academic record, exhibit leadership and initiative, and knock the case interviews out of the park by demonstrating the ability to approach a problem in a structured manner and break it into its components. (Reading this book might help too.)

LESSONS LEARNED AND IMPLEMENTATION ILLUSTRATIONS

By its nature, McKinsey has certain idiosyncrasies that have limited applicability outside its hallowed halls. For example, there is constant turnover within teams as employees move from project to project since each engagement typically lasts six months. Thus, there is always a large pool of available consultants to choose from, especially since team members can be plucked from any of McKinsey's offices worldwide. In recruiting, the Firm's reputation, high-profile client base, and generous pay provide a certain edge that is difficult to match in, say, a midsize manufacturing firm's recruiting efforts.

Even so, McKinsey's practices offer lessons that can help you with selecting and recruiting team members. Our interviews with

McKinsey alumni suggest three additional pieces of advice that will serve you well in this regard:

- Consider not just demonstrated ability, but potential ability.
- Appreciate the value of diversity.
- Apply structure to recruiting efforts.

Consider not just demonstrated ability, but potential ability. McKinsey's starting point for the selection process is a simple one: search for the best. Although this may sound intuitive, it is often forgotten in the workplace. Jim Bennett, in his leadership role at Key Corp., continued to make this a priority:

> A piece of standard McKinsey lore that has stuck with me in my post-McKinsey career involves the search for the very best people you can find. You should be on a relentless search for the best talent to suit the particular type of problem you are solving. We rely on formal evaluation tools that assess past experiences, strengths, and weaknesses. You also need to listen to the informal network as well; that may shed more light on the potential of the individual.

An individual's experience has long been a key criterion in recruiting efforts, whether it be with a particular industry, technology, or problem type. In certain situations, this orientation is necessary. You may need someone to hit the ground running on a project, and the team may not have time to learn an industry from scratch. McKinsey values experience and carefully screens candidates based on it.

The Firm also values potential ability, however, and in most cases, it prefers raw intellectual firepower to industry experience (there are, of course, exceptions, such as "practice specialist" positions). McKinsey believes that people can learn how to solve problems in a structured way, gather information about a company and industry, and present ideas, but it is darn near impossible to make someone more intelligent. Thus, the Firm seeks out bright individuals and trains them. Academic achievement and performance on case interviews weigh heavily in the selection process. Evan Grossman, now a partner at Hook Media, has adopted a similar policy in his new organization:

> One of the important things I learned at McKinsey was the importance of hiring smart people, as opposed to looking for people with tons of experience in a given area. It is important for us to hire people who can think logically. We do case-based interviews to assess their ability in this area and to ensure that they can be hypothesis driven.

McKinsey has managed to hire successful business consultants who influence quite a few of the world's largest, most successful companies. Many of their recruits had little to no actual experience in the area in which they are consulting. We believe that many recruiting efforts in other organizations overemphasize demonstrated performance in a narrowly defined area in preference to bright, trainable individuals who lack such prerequisites. By casting your net more widely, your organization may find future stars who only need a chance to demonstrate their potential.

Appreciate the value of diversity. These days, "diversity" is all the rage among recruiters, whether in business, government, or academia. When it comes to team selection, we're great believers in diversity, too. We depart, however, from the mainstream definition of diversity that values individuals based on their race, sex, religion, or dining preferences. How "diverse," after all, are two men—one who happens to be white, and the other black—both of whom prepped at Groton, majored in economics at Harvard, worked for two years on Wall Street, and received MBAs in finance from Wharton? Our book is about ways to enable more successful decision making in your organization, and that doesn't happen by counting individuals like beans. When we talk about valuing diversity, we don't mean some arbitrary program of affirmative action; we mean diversity of experience.

Take McKinsey, for example. It is hardly a diverse firm with regard to race, gender, or school backgrounds (the "average" McKinsey consultant in the United States is a white male with an MBA from a top-five business school). Over the past 10 years, though, the Firm has launched study after study on how to diversify its profile of consultants, and as a result, the mix is becoming much more diverse—and for good reason. The focus of this effort, however, has been to recruit more individuals with different backgrounds. For example, the Firm is hiring an increasing number of law students, Ph.D.s from all disciplines, and specialized industry hires.*

Dan Veto was a leader of recruiting in the Pittsburgh office of McKinsey. He claims that the real value of a team comes from diversity and the right balance of "background, enthusiasm, and strong intellect." He uses headhunters but is also open to hiring from "nontraditional" sources if that will help him assemble the best possible team.

What are the actual benefits of diversity on teams? Beyond simply broadening the skill mix of the team, diversity can bring fresh perspectives to bear on the problem and challenge assumptions that are too easily taken for granted. It can also make the

***Please remember that these are the views of the authors, not of McKinsey & Company. We don't speak for them, and they don't speak for us.**

whole problem-solving experience more interesting for the team. True diversity can strengthen the problem-solving process and enhance the development of individual team members.

Apply structure to recruiting efforts. As previously discussed, McKinsey follows a strictly formal recruiting process. The system includes a dedicated team of consultants and professionals who prepare detailed plans for each target school with itemized task lists and budgets. They crunch the numbers on candidates, track their status, and communicate frequently with those deemed hot prospects. Whether or not one makes it through the recruiting machine, one cannot dispute its efficiency and effectiveness. The Firm prides itself on avoiding "recruiting mistakes."

To improve your recruiting efforts, spend time developing a consistent recruiting process. For instance, Bill Ross is working to make recruiting at GE more systematic:

> GE has a tremendous amount of talent in its ranks but also a lot of variance. The recruiting effort, and the interview process specifically, could use some work. This was a great strength of McKinsey, and the result was an organization full of 100 percent top-notch high-performing individuals. Systematic, consistent recruiting helps in this regard. I have not yet had the opportunity to fully transfer these lessons to GE, but the need exists.

Not all companies need pay the same amount of attention and resources to recruiting as McKinsey. They may not hire as many people each year nor need the same amount of Olympian talent. There is no disputing, however, that employees are a critical element in every organization. Therefore you should apply some critical thinking to your recruiting strategy. The key lesson to learn from McKinsey in this regard is not one of formality, but rather the importance of forethought and consistency.

IMPLEMENTATION GUIDANCE

In thinking through your own organization, you must answer two key questions: Whom should we hire? And how should we hire them?

To answer the first question, start with your business needs. This goes beyond the basic job description. What is the most important task that this person will be responsible for? Although all positions involve numerous activities, assess the job using the elevator test (described in Chapter 5), and boil the job description down to a few sentences. For example, back at Acme Widgets, you've been put in charge of the search for a new purchasing manager for the Grommets Division. This person will be responsible for ensuring, at the lowest cost possible, the delivery of the bulk resins, intermediary plastics, and specialty polymers used in grommet production.

Devise a list of key attributes that relate to successful completion of the key tasks described in the first step. In the search for a purchasing manager, you are looking for telephone skills, negotiation ability, and a math or accounting background. Note that familiarity with grommets is not on the list, as you believe that Acme can adequately train the successful candidate in this technical aspect. You would have a harder time developing the listed skills if they were absent.

Now you know what kind of person you would like to hire. The next question is, how do you find the right person? You need a plan that identifies potential sources and details the tasks and resources required. For the Grommets Division, you decide that a two-person team, Joe and Robin, will handle the recruiting effort. They are to focus on recent math and accounting graduates from the local community college, preferably but not necessarily with some experience in manufacturing. They will also have a contingent budget for expanding the search to neighboring counties if they come up empty and the college agrees to give us a list of graduates from the past five years. You also place an advertisement in the local paper and run a posting on one of the leading Internet job search sites because you never know who might turn up.

Now, consider the team that the new purchasing manager will be joining, with respect to diversity. If everyone is of the same background and personality, you may miss innovation opportunities that more diverse combinations might stimulate. Say one candidate came from a different country; he may have new perspectives on interpersonal relations that might help in your dealings with suppliers. Another candidate with, say, computer-programming experience, might be able to improve your inventory management system. It's not enough to be open to candidates with varying backgrounds, however; you have to seek them out, and the suggestions in this section make a good starting point.

EXERCISES

- Identify your dream team. Start this exercise by completely ignoring anyone who works for you. Think of your most important tasks, and identify which ones require the help of others. Then, using the techniques described in this chapter, identify your specific business needs and lay out the ideal team to assist in accomplishing your and/or your department's (and ultimately your organization's) objectives. After the exercise, overlay the team with your current team and think through a strategy on how to best fill the gaps.
- Develop a recruiting plan. For this exercise, the starting point is an opening in your staff or a new position you would like to create. Actually document your recruiting plan, addressing the following areas: business needs, skill requirements, recruiting team, sources, and budget.

COMMUNICATION

Communication is one of the most important elements of effective team management. Teams can't function without it, yet its importance is often underestimated. There is no one best communication style, however, so in this section we explore a few general communication rules that should help as you develop your portfolio of communication skills.

THE McKINSEY WAY

At McKinsey the importance of communication was expressed by this principle: keep the information flowing.

Keep the information flowing. Information is power. Unlike other resources, information can actually increase in value as it is shared, to the benefit of everyone on your team. For your team to succeed, you have to keep the information flowing. You don't want someone to make a bad decision or say the wrong thing to a client just because he's out of the loop.

Teams communicate mainly through messages and meetings. Both should be kept brief and focused. In addition, remember the unscientific but powerful art of learning by walking around—random meetings to connect with team members outside of scheduled meetings.

LESSONS LEARNED AND IMPLEMENTATION ILLUSTRATIONS

All organizations develop a "communication culture" that governs the type and frequency of internal communication, and McKinsey is no exception. In most conversations at McKinsey, there are certain words and phrases you can expect to hear ("at the end of the day," "so what," and "client impact," for example). You'll also witness some common mannerisms (brief E-mails, grouping of issues in threes, responses to requests within 24 hours). In generating advice for other organizations, we feel it is more important to discuss general rules rather than McKinsey specifics:

- Remember that you have two ears and only one mouth.
- It's not just what you say, it's how you say it.
- Overcommunication is better than undercommunication.

Remember that you have two ears and only one mouth. Dean Dorman, who has worked for GE and two high-tech start-ups since leaving McKinsey, is never at a loss for words. His outgoing personality has served him well in his career and makes him fun to be around, but he has also learned the value of listening:

> In my latest position, as the president of Silver Oak, my listening skills are proving to be invaluable. I have served on the board for about a year, listening to the top-level discussions of business issues at the company. My first task as president was to conduct a "look, listen, and learn" tour involving two- to three-hour interviews with more than 40 key people in the organization to better understand what is going on. Before testing my hypotheses for a change program, it made sense to see exactly where people stood.

Most of us speak more than we listen. In managerial situations, this can cause problems. Not only do we risk making wrong decisions because we lack important facts, but we also induce resistance to change when the people involved feel their input is being ignored. Although chief executive officers and others recognize the importance of listening, how often do we formally cover the topic in academic curricula or corporate training programs?

Alan Barasky, now at one of the world's largest consulting and accounting firms, PricewaterhouseCoopers, took this lesson to heart:

> As I think of important lessons related to teamwork, three words come to mind: communicate, communicate, and communicate. Before, during, and after each major decision, milestone, project, or whatever. As I have learned, listening adds more value than talking.

What would this world be like if we spoke half as much as we listened? Who knows, less hot air might reduce global warming. Less noise pollution would be another benefit. We might also learn to pick our words carefully and just maybe become more thoughtful. We will discuss a few specific listening tips in the implementation ideas later in this chapter.

It's not just what you say, it's how you say it. Misunderstandings are a plague in today's workplace. The art of communication is full of inferences, innuendos, and nuances that make it difficult to convey our messages as we intend. Varying personality types, cultures, and agendas compound this problem.

To reduce miscommunication among its teams, McKinsey instituted a program of extensive interpersonal training. Three elements of the training were role-play interactions in first-year orientation, an advanced Interpersonal Skills Workshop (ISW) in the second or third year, and extensive use of the Myers-Briggs Type Indicator* for most engagement teams. These programs convey the importance of flexibility in verbal communication.

***Myers-Briggs Type Indicator (MBTI) is a copyrighted personality and communication assessment tool published by Consulting Psychological Press. Other tools exist as well, such as the Keirsey Temperament Sorter.**

We all have default communication styles rooted in, among other things, our upbringing, education, and training. Our word choices and tone of voice have great impact on our daily interactions with coworkers and clients. We need to develop a conscious understanding of our communication style—and sometimes change it. Formal programs, such as those used at McKinsey, can assist in that and help us develop a portfolio of communication skills. Those around us—our parents, spouse, and friends—can help, too.

Lee Newman, the executive vice president of on-line product development at HR One, describes how he brought this tool into his new organization after leaving McKinsey:

> The ISW program at McKinsey had great impact on me. The training was invaluable in developing my strategy for getting the most out of people in the teamwork environment. One of the specific tools I brought over was the MBTI [Myers-Briggs Type Indicator]. We use this extensively, and it helps us ensure that we leverage diversity in personality types and work styles to our advantage.

By becoming more familiar with our own communication style and understanding that other people have their own, different styles, we can begin to see beyond the way people are saying things to listen to what they are actually saying.

Overcommunication is better than undercommunication. When grilling chicken, there is a point at which the meat is perfectly done. Too much flame and it's shoe leather; too little heat means a quick trip to the emergency room. So it is with communication; we often under- or overcommunicate our message, but we rarely get it just right. And just like chicken on the grill, it's better to err on the side of too much rather than too little.

Let's compare the costs of under- and overcommunication. Undercommunication leads to lack of information, which in turn leads to mistakes. It also hurts the morale of the team when members are out of the loop and feel alienated. Even when we think we're saving time by not passing on information, we often end up having to play catch-up later on.

Overcommunication generally costs less. Yes, busy executives get annoyed when you give them too much information, but the cost of that to the organization is low, unless it takes overcommunication to an extreme. The marginal cost of including additional people in the information flow is small, especially given the ease of modern communication tools such as E-mail, voice mail, and intranets.

Moreover, the costs of overcommunication are mostly "opportunity costs": executives who could be performing value-added tasks have to spend incrementally more time filtering and assimilating information. Compare this with the value-destroying potential of undercommunication—clients or customers lost, accidents, lawsuits—and you can see why we say that more information is better than less. Of course, there are limits to this hypothesis, and you should assess each situation carefully. But in general, if you must err, do so on the side of overcommunication.

IMPLEMENTATION GUIDANCE

What specific steps can you take to improve communication in your organization? First, formalize listening training. In our survey of McKinsey alumni, we found that, in general, their new organizations offered considerably less interpersonal skills training than McKinsey does. Granted, not all companies are in a knowledge industry per se, but corporate training is increasingly becoming a source of competitive advantage. The amount spent on corporate training is huge, yet only a small portion of that training is in listening. Still, it is available. External consultants with expertise in listening or organizational behavior can help diagnose the state of communication within a firm. McKinsey regularly uses external consultants in this capacity.

Second, launch a personality profile program as part of your organization's human resource effort. As a first step in that direction, find the right tool for your organization. McKinsey uses Myers-Briggs, and most new consultants (and even their spouses or significant others) receive this training very early in their careers. The tool is extremely helpful in assessing one's baseline personality and communication style. Specifically, it measures the interaction type, problem-solving approach, and sensitivity. You can use the tool for a project team or department to assess the differences among personalities and identify strategies for dealing with conflict.

EXERCISES

- Conduct a Myers-Briggs evaluation on yourself (and your spouse if you like). You can visit the Consulting Psychological Press website for information on the MBTI at www.cpp-db.com. Find your personality type and understand the default communication style you possess. Consider the best strategies for dealing with positive and negative interaction between you and your coworkers and/or your spouse. How can you expand your communication portfolio and develop more flexibility in dealing with others?

BONDING

The concept of team bonding is easy to understand yet often overlooked. Why? Perhaps it is that the nature of business is to drive forward with a relentless focus on results. We often find ourselves in tough team situations because we overvalued the end product and undervalued the process of getting it done. This section serves as a reminder of the importance of putting a little time and energy into team bonding—and a little is probably all that is needed.

THE McKINSEY WAY

Two lessons from McKinsey regard team bonding.

Take your team's temperature to maintain morale. No one likes to walk into a freezing-cold or a boiling-hot room. Taking the temperature is an analogy that stresses the importance of staying in touch with your team to maintain a sense of the level of motivation and enthusiasm during the often-challenging course of a project. People who attend to motivation levels should steer a steady course, inform all team members of project status and their respective contribution, treat everyone with respect, get to know each other, and feel others' pain.

A little team bonding goes a long way. When a team spends 14 hours a day, 6 days a week working together, the last thing team members want to do in their precious remaining time is go on a team outing to Disney World or to dinner at the most expensive restaurant in town. Some of that is OK, but the balance is important. Too much can be as bad as too little. Bonding can take place at work, too, so try to lighten up at times.

That said, when you do plan bonding events, be strategic. Focus on something that everyone will enjoy, and include significant others when possible.

LESSONS LEARNED AND IMPLEMENTATION ILLUSTRATIONS

More often than not, our alumni suggest that bonding is not the norm in their post-McKinsey positions. So rather than jump right in with the idea that retreats, fancy dinners, and family fun events are the way to go, they suggested a more conservative approach that still aims to increase performance through team bonding. This boiled down to two lessons:

- Spend time together (but not too much).
- Reward well.

Spend time together (but not too much). Dan Veto brought a high level of energy and new ideas for bonding to his new position as the head of the strategy group of Conseco:

> I am a believer in the need for team events, as we called them at McKinsey. This company and many others are less accustomed to that idea. It doesn't have to be that expensive. Even taking a dozen people out to dinner is relatively cheap in terms of the cost/benefit when you consider the impact on productivity and the morale boost of getting to know each other better. I believe in this so much that there have been instances when I have paid for events out of my own pocket.
>
> People take pictures at these things and put them up on their desks, which helps us build our own group identity. Some other departments are following suit but probably not enough of them.

Maybe they should. Other examples from alumni support Dan's basic premise that some fun time outside of work can pay major dividends and doesn't cost that much.

Bonding doesn't just have to be around a fun theme; you can also bond while getting something done. McKinsey combines incredible office retreats to exotic locations (usually involving a golf course, ski resort, or beach) with developmental programs. Kurt Lieberman, now at Reynolds & Reynolds, took this lesson to heart:

> One of the most effective tools I brought from McKinsey related to team bonding and problem solving. I take the top two levels of my organization off-site every other month for a half day. Most of the work is done in subteams with each team reporting its results. Sometimes each subteam solves the same problem, sometimes not, but bonding always takes place.

This example shows how team exercises can be work-oriented and still contribute to bonding. You don't have to go anywhere fancy; just a new location can make a world of difference.

Our alumni also counseled moderation. In the words of comedian Steven Wright, "You can't have everything; where would you put it?"* Too much bonding can overload the team. It even drove one alumna to leave McKinsey:

> The bonding expectations at McKinsey were tough at times. In fact, this element of the lifestyle was one that I was ultimately unable to resolve. The Firm expected far too much outside of regular client work, such as recruiting events, team dinners, Practice Development, etc. I worked too hard on my client projects to be excited about leaving my family

*Steven Wright is not, as far as the authors are aware, a McKinsey alumnus.

> to go on a firm retreat or to spend an evening out entertaining prospective analysts. The extracurricular demands spiraled out of control because no one at a senior level focused on how much of a burden [this expectation] was. The irony is that the more successful one was, the more of the extra work one had to do, and therefore the more likely one was to leave the Firm.

It may be this concern that leads certain companies to avoid planning social events altogether. We advise against that. These events offer performance-enhancing activities that simply cannot be replicated in most existing work environments. Our suggestion: Plan few events, but plan them strategically. Focus on their timing, type, and participant lists to ensure the highest impact at the lowest cost.

Reward well. Steve Anderson, president and CEO of Acorn Systems, a technology consulting company, found that his new culture was even more intense than McKinsey's. Still, he told us, the rewards were greater as well:

> Acorn is more intense than McKinsey, and thus we have to work hard not only to build company morale, but also to foster team bonding. Our teams hardly get any sleep on the road. So, to top it off, we have very nice, long dinners, stay in comfortable hotels, and party hard. It is amazing how consultants thrive in this intense culture. We also have other rewards such as regular office dinners and Fridays in the office for everybody. *Nobody* works on weekends. We stole almost all these winning reward philosophies from McKinsey.

Of course, not all organizations are this intense (thank goodness). Different types of rewards will work in different companies. As examples, some alumni mentioned bonuses, extra days off, trophies, and publications as rewards in their new organizations. These rewards need not be financial. Often, simple but widespread recognition programs work even more effectively than financial incentives for motivating performance.

IMPLEMENTATION GUIDANCE

When designing a program of bonding activities in your organization, bear in mind two things: culture and resources.

As with so many management topics, the context of the culture of your organization (or department or team, as cultures can vary widely within organizations) will play a major role in how best to promote bonding. There are so many variations in norms and acceptable behavior—a team night out at a typical Silicon Alley dot-com might be scandalous at, say, Proctor and Gamble—that we wouldn't dare to suggest exactly which type of activity would work best for you. Still, we believe that most organizations could benefit from a bit of loosening up—not that they should forget about strategic planning or financial controls, just that people should enjoy themselves a little more in the workplace. We also suggest that you consider some events beyond the annual company picnic or golf outing: go-carting, bowling, skiing, paintball, anything to take people out of their routine and help them bond.

Once you've come up with the ultimate bonding program, you still have to get the resources, that is, the money, to pay for it. Paintball for 300 people isn't cheap. Frankly, we assume that a certain amount of bonding improves performance within the organization. This seems intuitive to us and, since quite a number of companies spend a lot of money on such activities, to many corporations around the world. Nevertheless, if your organization doesn't devote many resources to bonding, then you will probably have to make a case for the benefits of bonding that will convince whoever controls your organization's purse strings.

How would you go about this? If the decision makers in your organization respond well to qualitative arguments, then you could put together a proposal based on the intuitive argument that bonding leads to better performance. If, on the other hand, your culture values quantitative arguments, then put together an analysis of the financial benefits of enhanced performance. If you can find an example of best practice in your industry or organization—for example, one business unit that is especially good at bonding—use it to bolster your argument. You might also try to launch a modest pilot program. If you can show that the program yields benefits via improved performance, then you have a launching pad from which to expand your bonding program throughout the organization.

As you plan your activities, remember the moderation message. For example, plan just a few key events over the course of a year. Involve as many people in the planning process as possible (even send surveys for ideas). The exposure will increase interest and eventual buy-in. Another helpful tip is to evaluate employees' satisfaction with different types of events and continually focus on the few events that are most appreciated. Finally, don't forget to have fun.

EXERCISES

- Assess the rewards system in your organization. Create a list of all of the reward mechanisms your organization uses. Be sure to include financial and nonfinancial rewards in the summary, but track them separately. Then rank the items on each list, using the following question as your decision criterion: How much does this mechanism mean to me in terms of motivation and team bonding? If possible, have others in your team or department go through the exercise as well. Try to identify a few reward mechanisms that are most powerful. If you are in a position to do so, consider whether you can request more resources to ensure that the most powerful mechanisms stay in place.

- Develop a social plan for your team or department. Use the advice in the Implementation Guidance of this section as a starting point. It may be helpful to include others in the planning process. Focus on identifying the types of activities and timing that would be most appropriate for your organization. Include as many details as possible, and refer to this plan as you launch your program.

DEVELOPMENT

We believe that to be satisfying, a job should provide ample opportunities for the employee to develop. This development comes not only from experience but also via a process of objective setting, performance assessment, and feedback that helps the employee to meet both her career goals and the objectives of the organization.

The original outline of this book—our initial hypotheses, if you will—did not have a development section. After reviewing our alumni interview notes, however, the topic surfaced as one of the most important lessons that alumni took with them—and one they are actively implementing in their new organizations. By the end of this section, we hope that you will realize that one of the most important responsibilities you have in managing teams is ensuring the individual development of team members.

THE McKINSEY WAY

McKinsey intensively trains its first-class consultants to solve business problems. Development at McKinsey is so ingrained in the culture that it has become second nature.

LESSONS LEARNED AND IMPLEMENTATION ILLUSTRATIONS

We dissected development at McKinsey and interviewed alumni to find ways that other organizations can evaluate and enhance their development programs. Our McKinsey alumni were very clear in articulating how they have transferred McKinsey lessons in development into their new organizations. They gave us two broad guidelines:

- Set high expectations.
- Evaluate regularly, and make it balanced.

Set high expectations. At the beginning of our interview with Jim Bennett, who was in charge of retail banking at Key Corp. at the time, high performance aspirations became the central topic of the discussion:

> The single most important McKinsey tool I have in my new position is the power to set very, very high performance aspirations and drive the organization to achieve them. For example, my team and I established a $100 million cost reduction target and made it public. Quite a goal, but we are going after it aggressively, and it is amazing what you can accomplish when you do it in a "take no prisoners" manner.

What applies to the organization also holds for the individuals within it. High expectations lead to high results; low expectations yield low results. Development equals change, something many are uncomfortable with. By setting high goals (with implicitly high rewards for their achievement), managers help overcome the inertia that results from the fear of change. Setting a "stretch" target that appears—at least, at first—unreachable forces the employees and the organization to deploy all their creativity and energy toward reaching the goal. Exploring new ideas and options ("thinking outside the box" in MBA parlance) can be a liberating experience for the individual and a profitable one for the organization.

Evaluate regularly, and make it balanced. Feedback is a double-edged sword. On one hand, we have a strong interest in finding out what people think of us, as a means both to improve ourselves and to feed our egos. On the other hand, feedback can make us uncomfortable when it forces us to confront our weaknesses. Handled properly, feedback is one of the most important development tools around, and McKinsey offers some good lessons on doing it well.

The Firm has instituted a number of formal developmental tools that may transfer well to your organization. First, each consultant is assigned a formal mentor, the Development Group Leader (DGL). This person is usually at the partner level and is responsible for monitoring a consultant's progress as she moves through the ranks of the Firm. The DGL has access to all of a consultant's performance reviews and discusses them in detail with other members of the engagement team.

The Firm also uses a formal evaluation form that is completed by the EM or partner for each consultant after each project. It includes a grid of key skill areas (analytical, interpersonal, leadership, etc.) with specific expectations as to where a consultant at each level should be in each area. Certain McKinsey offices have implemented 360-degree feedback programs. In these programs, each consultant is evaluated by anyone who comes in contact with the consultant, including subordinates, peers, supervisors, and even administrative personnel. Many teams at McKinsey also use Team Evaluation Performance Reviews where they explicitly evaluate their performance working together. There is no shortage of feedback at McKinsey; in fact, some may argue that there is too much (as we discuss at the end of this section).

McKinsey alumni found these techniques very effective. Some of them miss that feedback in their current organizations. Ron O'Hanley, now the president of Mellon Institutional Asset Management, reflects on his attempts to develop similarly intense feedback channels in his organization:

> Real teams have open, unimpaired feedback loops. This is very hard in a traditional corporate hierarchy. Open feedback, particularly about me, has become a way of life around here.

Barbara Goose, now the vice president and associate marketing director at Digitas, brought some of the specific tools with her:

> I have used tools similar to the Team Evaluation Performance Review effectively with my teams. Other organizations that I have been a part of tend not to be as thorough with team selection, evaluation, and development. The Development Group Leader (at McKinsey) played a large role in this—and that is often missing at other places. You really felt at McKinsey like you had an advocate.

This hard-hitting, constant evaluation and development advice is not for everyone. Even though we are all on a developmental journey, the bumps along the road can be uncomfortable at times. One of the areas that some say McKinsey misses is the balance. When it comes to comments, there are two considerations: quantity and type (i.e., positive or negative).

The quantity issue comes down to how many comments are enough. Giving too few comments leaves employees in the dark, relying on their self-evaluative skills to lead them to proper developmental moves. Too many comments also can have a negative effect on motivation. The employee may feel that there is too much pressure and become so consumed with the evaluation that other job responsibilities become secondary.

IMPLEMENTATION GUIDANCE

As we said at the beginning of this section, development is a continuous cycle. When you are in charge of someone's development—when you are a mentor—you have to set objectives for that person that meet the needs of both the organization and the individual. Then you must assess the employee's performance and provide feedback. Based on that feedback, you set new objectives, thus starting the cycle over again.

The first step, as so often in this book, is to identify your organizational objectives. What are the primary tasks for which your employees (or you, for that matter) are responsible? In consulting, it boils down to analytical skills, teamwork, and presentation. Develop aggressive target expectations in each area for everyone in your organization. Consider also the goals of those you are mentoring. You should meet with them to establish their expectations of their role and career and incorporate those expectations into whatever objectives you set.

Next, consider how you communicate these expectations to employees in the organization. Is there a consistent and formal program, or is it loose, relying on word of mouth and advice from more-experienced employees? Both types of systems have strengths and weaknesses. The choice between them comes down to the culture of your organization. Chances are you know which method suits your corporate culture best.

Some organizations are particularly hard to change because their employees have developed routines and even entire personalities around the formal and informal procedures and incentive programs in their organization.

Performance assessment should meet three criteria. It should be objective, be based on expectations that were set in advance, and account only for events that were within the control of the person you are mentoring. Objectivity is paramount if the mentoring process is to be of any benefit to the employee. You won't necessarily like everyone you mentor, but you musn't let personal feelings get in the way of doing your job. In addition, if you don't communicate your expectations ahead of time, the individual will be flying blind; you can't expect him to meet goals under such circumstances. And don't blame the person you mentor for things beyond his control: if the client goes bankrupt or the economy plunges into recession, that's unlikely to be his fault.

Finally, think about the frequency and type of feedback in your organization. Many people automatically assume that development comments need to be negative, pointing out what is wrong and then suggesting ways to change. Positive comments, however, play a critical role in development as well.

Let's explore the impact of positive and negative comments on performance, using a graph to illustrate a hypothesis based on our own experience. As shown in Figure 6-1, the performance curves vary based on the nature of the comment. For simplicity, think negative or positive; a negative comment points out a weakness, and a positive comment recognizes a strength. By the way, negative comments that are communicated in a nice tone are *not* positive comments.

The messages from this chart and hypothesis are as follows. First, a few negative comments are important to influence performance. The absence of negative comments does not assist in development (and if we look hard enough, all of us have areas we can develop). It doesn't take too long, however, for the slope of the negative-comment curve to reverse. As humans, we can only absorb and appreciate a certain number of negative comments before we begin to lose motivation and become demoralized. The positive comments represent a more gradual slope, meaning a few more positive comments are necessary to truly influence performance. However, the impact of more positive comments continues for a longer period of time. Eventually the positive comments reach a "B.S. point," the level at which the comments appear superficial or unbelievable.

Overall, the message of this graph is that balanced feedback is best. It is important to point out weaknesses and development opportunities but to avoid going overboard and making every comment a "suggestion for improvement." Positive comments play

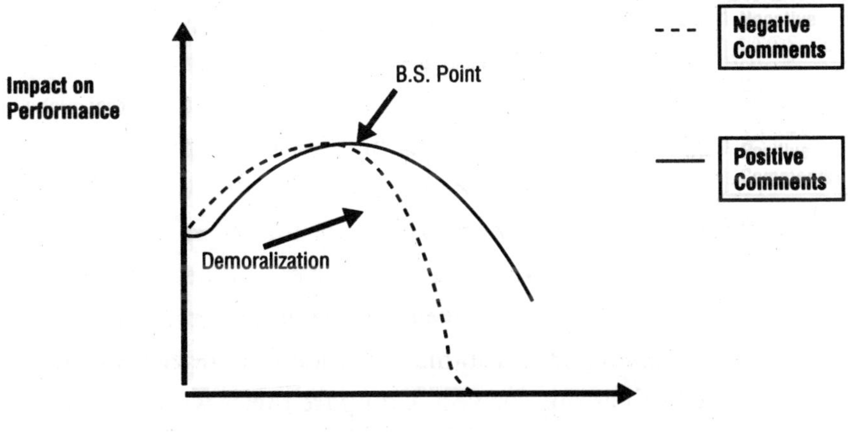

Figure 6-1. Feedback Impact Model

a critical role as well, and all of us could use a few more *way to gos* and *attaboys*. Again, balance is key. Too much praise can have detrimental effects as well if it appears insincere—especially if it never identifies any areas for improvement.

EXERCISES

- Take a self-development journey. Examine your own developmental needs. We recommend involving others (direct reports, peers, spouse, friends, etc.) in the process. For help with this process, try one of the packaged tools that have been developed for this use (such as those available from the Center for Creative Leadership and the Franklin Covey Institute). Your goal: an honest assessment of your strengths and weaknesses, not just as you perceive them, but also as others perceive them. In addition to identifying your development portfolio, you should also identify one or two major aspects to focus on (if you try for more, you may hit the demoralization level).
- Identify the development needs of your direct reports. You interact with them every day, but have you spent much time actually reflecting on their development needs? And try to think from their perspective, not just yours. Think of the person holistically, not just in terms of your requirements. Create a list of positives and negatives (opportunities for improvement, if you prefer) for each of your direct reports. You may ask them to create their own list, as well as one for you. Compare theirs with the list you made. Try to avoid doing this over lunch, lest a food fight break out.

CONCLUSION

The study of leadership and team management has received significant attention in academic and practitioner study over the past 50 years, and for good reason—a little improvement in this area can yield large results. Accordingly, most of the concepts presented in this chapter are not new. Instead, our focus has been on pulling out the nuggets of wisdom that McKinsey consultants offer, based on their extensive experience in teams.

Team management is often more of an art than a science, and the specific recommendations in this chapter may not apply in all situations. Even so, the general themes of careful selection, constant communication, selective bonding, and purposeful development should serve us all well.

FINANCIAL AND PERFORMANCE RATIOS (INDUSTRY AVERAGES)

- *Almanac of Business and Industrial Financial Ratios*—This source contains tables of ... ratios for more than 200 ... categories in ... included in this work ... that is close to the ... *Statement Studies* and ... are similar ... find them in ... *Corporation* ... industry averages ... returns filed ... are drawn ... ments, and other sources ... there are several ...
- *Standard and ...* at for ... are ... pages long ... bonds, a ... since the ... financial ... in the industry ... includes a ... pany in this ... list of additional ... reference ... libraries.

7

MANAGING YOUR CLIENT

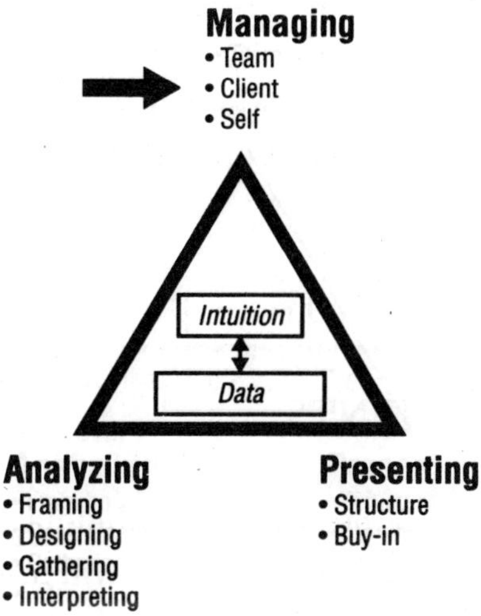

Who is your client? Depending on your circumstances, it could be a customer, vendor, supplier, boss, CEO, shareholder, or any combination thereof. If your business is to succeed, you have to put the client first. This tenet lies at the heart of McKinsey's vision of itself as a professional service firm.

Dealing with clients can be a wonderful, enriching experience (in both the monetary and psychic senses), a true win-win situation. More often than not, however, it is a challenging and frustrating effort. If you're in sales, you know just how difficult it is to be on the constant hunt for new business. Even if you're not in sales, if you're in the business world, then you have a client somewhere whom you have to satisfy.

In this chapter we will look at three areas of client management: *obtaining*, *maintaining*, and *retaining*. The concept of obtaining clients is clear—to have clients to manage, you have to get them in the first place. Client maintenance is the steps you take to keep your client engaged in and happy with your progress during the course of a project. We distinguish this from retention—the fine art of getting follow-on work from a client after a project is finished. As you will see, the experiences of McKinsey alumni in these areas can help you build an expanding portfolio of happy clients.

OBTAINING CLIENTS

This section focuses on the tools and techniques that will help you win new client business. The lessons you will read here are unlikely to show up in traditional sales books and journals for one fundamental reason: we believe that the best selling is done by not selling.

THE McKINSEY WAY

McKinsey has a unique approach to obtaining clients.

How to sell without selling. If you ask a McKinsey consultant how the Firm sells its services, you will be told, in a slightly haughty tone, that McKinsey doesn't sell. That's only partly true.

In fact, McKinsey sells, but it uses an indirect approach. Instead of cold calls and mass mailings, the Firm relies almost exclusively on existing relationships to generate new business. Many of McKinsey's engagements are follow-on work (a fancy term describing an additional project for a client after one is finished). To build relationships, the Firm markets: it publishes books and articles; it performs extensive community service (which often has the added benefit of allowing McKinsey consultants to rub elbows with the corporate titans who populate so many charitable boards); and it sponsors topical presentations and workshops. All of these efforts serve to get McKinsey's name out there—if its reputation isn't enough already—and broadens the Firm's network of corporate decision makers, any of whom might be in a position to call their local McKinsey office with their business problems.

Be careful what you promise: structuring an engagement. In the words of George W. Bush, "A promise made, is a promise kept." Over the years, McKinsey has learned how important it is to make good on its promises. Unfortunately, even McKinsey sometimes forgets that it can only fulfill a promise if the promise is reasonable. Bear this in mind when laying down the boundaries of your project—don't overpromise because you're bound to underdeliver, which is no way to get follow-on business. Instead, balance the demands of the client with the capabilities of your team. If the client wants you to do more, you can always start a second project once the first is done.

LESSONS LEARNED AND IMPLEMENTATION ILLUSTRATIONS

At first glance, one may think that obtaining clients in a consulting environment varies dramatically from other industries. Our alumni who are now in other industries, however, claim that McKinsey lessons also helped them. Based on our interviews with them, we have isolated two particular considerations:

- Identify the client.
- Create a pull, rather than a push, demand.

Identify the client. Does this sound intuitive? Perhaps it is easier said than done, especially at the level of understanding that is necessary to ensure successful interaction. Take the government, for example. You might think that in this traditionally hierarchical, structured organization identifying your client and your client's needs would be simple. Not so says Sylvia Mathews, who culminated eight years of public service as the Deputy Director of the Office of Management and Budget in the Clinton administration:

> This is a place where identifying your client is not always that easy—it is by no means transparent. For example, I certainly don't have just one client. The president and vice president are Client Number One. Then there are the different cabinet departments, each with various individuals wanting to be the point person. There are also interagency teams that must be managed. Then there is Congress, which is a critical client since it passes the laws that make things happen.

The challenge is not just identifying your client—you must then go deeper. Each client has a particular agenda that you must consider and balance. Mathews describes the best way to handle this as "constant negotiation." Knowledge of the true identity of your clients and a strategy for handling competing sets of needs is not an easy task but is one to which you should dedicate time and attention up front.

Create a pull rather than a push demand. Bill Ross left McKinsey as an engagement manager, just below the partner ranks, and never had to spend too much time worrying about selling new engagements. When he moved to GE, even though he didn't have outside clients, he realized that he had to start selling:

> My client is really the CEO of this business. I have more clients as well—the managers of specific business units. We have to sell. The products I'm selling are my ideas. In many cases, I'm trying to get them to think differently and put my thoughts into their thoughts—to get them engaged with my ideas, so that when they have a problem, they turn to me. This requires an up-front investment of resources and time. That's the secret—to create awareness of your offering so that selling becomes less of a push and more of a pull.

This is the practical application of the McKinsey approach to indirect selling. Rather than sticking a foot in the door and barging in cold, build up a reputation and let it preceed you. Put the client in a position to recognize that you're the one who can fill her need—then she'll call you.

Effective selling, then, becomes the identification of client needs and the building of expertise around them. Once you've done that, you can begin the subtle art of indirect selling by making people aware of what you know. Since you have done your research up front, you don't need to be explicit in your sales effort. Just allow the potential client to make the connection between his need and your expertise—as the voice said in the movie *Field of Dreams*, "If you build it, they will come." Just make sure they can find you.

IMPLEMENTATION GUIDANCE

It's time to return to our team at Acme Widgets. Lukas, the newly minted Grommets purchasing manager (you hired him in Chapter 6), has just finished his introductory training course and is ready to start work. Unfortunately, no one has told him exactly who his client is. He knows that he reports to Madeleine, the vice president of production, but he has a feeling he also answers to several more people. To get a handle on the problem, he sits down and makes a list of everyone with whom he interacts and updates this list over time. He lists the specific demands they have of him and when. He also identifies exactly how his efforts help them get their jobs done. For kicks, he also lists two adjectives that describe the personality of each person.

When he analyzes his own position, he sees that he does much more than just order raw materials. For example, for Maddie, his boss (Ms. Trott to him), he ensures that inventory is kept low so that inventory costs and write-offs are kept to a minimum. Grace and Zach, two production supervisors who use the majority of his parts, look to Lukas to keep adequate stocks of both raw materials and spare parts to avoid a break in their manufacturing schedules. His administrative assistant, Mike, wants to grow in his job and do much more than just answer the phone. Thinking strategically about his clients and their needs, Lukas realizes that he has the potential to add value for his organization through improved management of inventory information; he decides to invest in a new scheduling software package with terminal linkage to the production supervisors and cost report generation on a daily basis to his boss. He also sends Mike on a special training program to learn how to run the software.

Lukas is off to a good start and he is quickly building a reputation for innovative solutions. He did so by thinking carefully about exactly who his clients are and what they need. He then developed an innovative solution based on their needs and made them aware of its capabilities. They began coming to him for additional information, and it wasn't long before Lukas was promoted to the knowledge management department as a manufacturing information liaison.

EXERCISES

- What is your sales offering? Identify an important issue you have been working on that has faced internal resistance. Next, think through the sources of resistance—where are the roadblocks? Instead of trying to convince people of the merits of your particular issue, identify an opportunity to share something you know well to help them with their current problem. Make it a credible, fact-based deliverable that increases your exposure and garners general support.

MAINTAINING CLIENTS

Now that the client is in hand and established, we move to a new stage in the relationship—maintenance. As with any relationship, this requires careful consideration of the wants, needs, and desires of all parties.

THE McKINSEY WAY

There are quite a few McKinsey lessons dedicated to this topic—hardly surprising given their obsession with client service—and rather than summarize them one-by-one, we will discuss their key points all together:

- Engage the client in the process
- Always look over your shoulder
- Keep the client team on your side
- Learn to deal with liability client team members
- Pluck the low-hanging fruit
- Get buy-in throughout the organization

Two underlying themes emerge from these lessons. The first is that proactive steps must be taken to manage client involvement: keep them involved through active participation, not just periodic updates; deal with troublesome team members in a direct, developmental manner (or work around the worst cases); and rejoice in small victories that help win the war. Like the management lessons from the previous chapter, mediating client involvement is best considered a separate task that requires special attention and thinking on your part as the client manager. The other theme centers on consideration of the clients: work around their schedule, send agendas ahead of time, don't take too much of their time, appreciate what they have done, and keep client data strictly confidential.

LESSONS LEARNED AND IMPLEMENTATION ILLUSTRATIONS

The "client involvement" theme resonates with McKinsey alumni as they move into their post-McKinsey positions. The primary lesson from their implementation efforts simply focuses on becoming creative and proactive: create involvement opportunities.

Create involvement opportunities. Shyam Giridharadas left McKinsey to found and run his own consulting firm, Prism Consulting International. He learned that delivering consistent high-quality work was not enough; client involvement was critical:

> Fact-based, creative problem solving and objective, intellectually honest recommendations are the hallmarks of an excellent management consultant, but this is only half of the equation. Consulting work is most effectively undertaken in the client's own backyard. It becomes extremely important to integrate client team members at all levels within the orga-

> nization and not just with the office of the CEO. It is vital for the "McKinsey Mind" not to confine itself to brilliant problem solving but to communicate incessantly throughout the engagement process to integrate effectively and to create a following.

Shyam pinpoints the locus of problem solving: it is best done in the "client's backyard." For example, more and more manufacturing companies' research and development departments include customers in the process, often sending scouts to witness how the products are actually used and how they can be improved. Another important element to successful integration is "incessant communication." Just as we favor overcommunication among team members, so too do we recommend keeping your client well fed with relevant information.

IMPLEMENTATION GUIDANCE

In company boardrooms and academic classrooms, the buzz today is about changing organizational boundaries. Some believe that the days of the massive organization may come to an end as "knowledge workers" broker their services on an open, fluid market with continually changing group lines. Two of the forces driving this potentially seismic change are new technologies, especially in wired and wireless communication, and globalization. Although we will leave the forecasting to the experts—such as they are—it is clear that assumptions about the role of customers are changing.

Today's buyers are much more sophisticated and have greater requirements. This is why many companies (including consulting firms) have changed their approach to include them in the value-creation process, from initial design to final implementation. Are there opportunities where you can go beyond the almost expected consideration of the client to the full team member view of the client? Strive not to report or deliver to them but to jointly create with them.

EXERCISES

- Create a client development plan. Think of your most important client. How involved is this client in the design and/or delivery of your product or service? Think creatively about any opportunities that exist where the client can actually come into your organization to assist in the process. Be radical. Before you send an invitation, however, make sure that you can articulate anticipated benefit of their involvement (for you and the client).

RETAINING CLIENTS

The final section of this chapter is dedicated to finding ways to keep your client for the long term. This has become a mainstay of the McKinsey strategy as the Firm focuses on developing deep relationships with the key players at the Fortune 100 companies and megacorporations around the world.

THE McKINSEY WAY

The McKinsey client model is relationship driven and the key to retention is ultimately meeting and exceeding client expectations. Let's review how they do it.

Be rigorous about implementation. This lesson took McKinsey quite a while to fully understand and implement. For a long time, the Firm was known for outstanding idea generation but poor implementation. Translation—lots of insight-laden reports gathering dust on corporate bookshelves. To avoid the same fate for your ideas, focus on the ability of the client to implement your solution. In addition, before you head off to the next problem, present a clear implementation plan that includes exactly what should be done, by whom, and when. This applies not only to consulting projects but also to internal projects that hinge on future activities for eventual value generation.

LESSONS LEARNED AND IMPLEMENTATION ILLUSTRATIONS

Focus your client retention efforts on the long term. Base every decision on how it will affect the long-term relationship with your client. In the case of McKinsey, one of the most important elements of ensuring long-term successful relationships is the Firm's ability to generate lasting change. For some time, implementation was considered McKinsey's weak spot. As its clients became more sophisticated, the Firm realized that this couldn't last. They took steps to improve not just their ability to devise a course of change but to make change happen. Our alumni have taken those lessons into the world beyond McKinsey and used them to build their new organizations and businesses. Their recommendations:

- Share and then transfer responsibility
- Make the client a hero

Share and then transfer responsibility. At some point, you have to learn to let go. When it comes to client involvement, one of the common arguments holding back such efforts is a concern over quality or efficiency. The problem with this orientation is that it focuses too much on the short term. The first step is to take the risk of some inefficiency in order to involve the client in a greater role. Bob Garda, now a faculty member of Duke University's Fuqua School of Business, elaborates on the benefit of sharing the decision-making process:

> When it comes to client management, I always remember a phrase from McKinsey—"cover from behind." That means, when you get some analysis done, you go to the person who gave you the data and let them help you interpret it. You build a lot of friends and you build a lot of allies.

This also relates to previously discussed themes of client buy-in. The premise is that clients (internal or external) who were involved in the problem-solving process make the best advocates. This method also ensures that an eventual transfer takes place, which was facilitated by the sharing of the overall process throughout.

Make the client a hero. Jeff Sakaguchi, now a partner at Accenture, learned a valuable lesson about the importance of including clients in the problem-solving process so that they can share in the glory:

> One area where McKinsey and Accenture excel is matching client structure. We recognize how important it is to have a steering committee at the top, but you have also got to design a complementary team that involves the client at all levels. Clients are so much more capable than many people believe. The key is to introduce accountability and exposure. They will be just as committed to achieving success. They will take ownership, and it is our job to help them get the job done.

If you view your job as a challenge to help clients win, rather than focusing on how you win, good things will happen. This does not suggest that you should abandon all basic profitability considerations, but it does suggest thinking of others first as you make daily decisions. As Jeff described above, give your clients more credit and give them opportunities to succeed—with you.

IMPLEMENTATION GUIDANCE

The tricky part in this section is not the goal of client involvement but the specifics of where to include the client in the process—or, perhaps more aptly, where to exclude him. For this we have two suggestions.

First, pluck some low-hanging fruit with a pilot program. Pick a particular product or division with a single meaningful client and identify areas where the client can safely become involved in the efforts designed to meet that particular client's needs. Once you have gained some momentum you can broaden the effort throughout the organization. Second, control the process. Some clients may take the proverbial inch and turn it into a mile. Be very clear about the scope of the involvement—that includes goals, timing, and exact expectations.

EXERCISES

- Benchmark client involvement activity. Pick an industry different from your own. Identify the extent of client involvement in the delivery portion of this industry. Where are the opportunities for involvement and how many companies are actively utilizing clients as described in this chapter? How would you increase the involvement if you were in that industry?

CONCLUSION

McKinsey works hard to involve its clients in the creation of change in their organizations. Most industries can learn a valuable lesson by considering how to more actively involve clients in their delivery efforts as well. Moreover, we, as individuals, stand to learn a lesson or two about the importance of putting others first.

In the next chapter, however, we will look at ways to put another, very important person first—you.

8

MANAGING YOURSELF

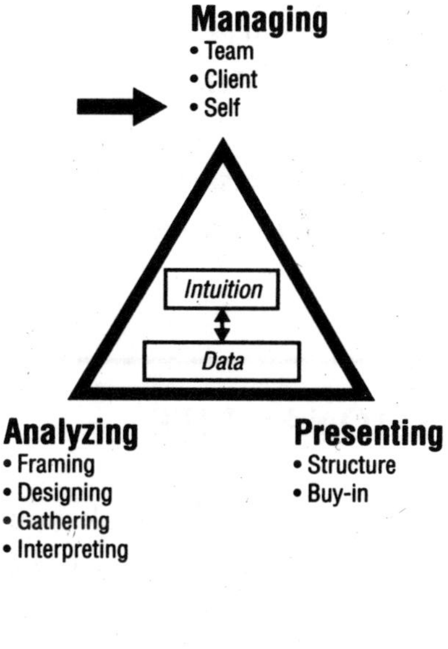

Among themselves, McKinsey-ites often quip that the true Firm hierarchy is Client, Firm, You. Notice that you come last—some would say distantly so. It is therefore appropriate that in this last chapter we discuss a few techniques for self-management, both professional and personal, as practiced by McKinsey alumni.

The term *self-management* (along with its cousins *self-help* and *self-improvement*) means different things to different people. The world's bookstores bristle with titles purporting to help you get ahead, get organized, get happy, get romance, and get thin. Some of them may even come good on their promises.

Our goals are more modest. In the course of our research, we have come across a few lessons that may help you be more successful in your career or balance the competing demands of workplace and home. We pass them on to you in the hope that they may prove helpful. We make no promises.

More than any other topic in this book, this subject permits no "one best way." We are all, by definition, unique individuals, and the strategy that helps Tom balance life and career may do nothing at all for Dick—and may prove an absolute disaster for Harriet. Having said that, the McKinsey alumni who have helped us throughout this book have a wealth of life and professional experience and are almost universally successful. They must know a few things about getting ahead while maintaining one's sanity.

YOUR PROFESSIONAL LIFE

We assume that anybody reading this book would like to get a little closer to the top of the corporate ladder, if you have not already reached it. In this section, we discuss a few techniques for making that progression easier and, perhaps, quicker.

THE McKINSEY WAY

McKinsey-ites had a lot to say about climbing the Firm's greasy pole of success.

Find your own mentor. Take advantage of others' experience by finding someone senior in your organization to be your mentor. Even though some firms have formal mentoring programs, you would still do well to take the initiative to find someone to steer you through the twists and turns of corporate life.

Hit singles. This isn't a call to commit battery on the unwed, it's a metaphor from baseball. You can't do everything, so don't try. Just do what you're supposed to do, and get it right. It's impossible to do everything yourself all the time. If you do manage that feat once, you raise unrealistic expectations from those around you. Then, when you fail to meet those expectations, you'll have difficulty regaining your credibility. Getting on base consistently is much better than trying to hit a home run and striking out nine times out of ten.

Make your boss look good. If you make your boss look good, your boss will make you look good. You do that by doing your job to the best of your ability and letting your boss know everything you know when she needs to know it. Make sure she knows where you are, what you are doing, and what problems you may be having. However, don't overload her with information. In return for your efforts, she should praise your contributions to the organization.

An aggressive strategy for managing hierarchy. Sometimes, to get things done, you have to assert yourself. If you face a vacuum in power or responsibility, fill it before someone else does. This strategy can be risky; the more so, the more hierarchical your organization. Be sensitive to the limits of others' authority, and be ready to retreat quickly if necessary.

A good assistant is a lifeline. Having someone to perform the myriad support tasks required by a busy executive—typing, duplicating, messaging, and filing, to name but a few—can be exceptionally valuable. Whether the people who perform these tasks are called secretaries, assistants, interns, or simply junior staff, treat them well. Be clear about your wants and needs, and give them opportunities to grow in their responsibilities and careers, even if they are not on the executive track.

LESSONS LEARNED AND IMPLEMENTATION ILLUSTRATIONS

While many things change for McKinsey-ites when they leave the Firm, the stresses of life in the business world remain, or even increase, improbable as that may sound. McKinsey-ites are nothing if not resourceful, however, and they've come up with ways to survive and thrive despite the rigors of corporate life. Our alumni were happy to share some of their career management techniques:

- Delegate around your limitations.
- Make the most of your network.

Delegate around your limitations. Throughout this book, we've advocated understanding the limitations of others: your client, your organization, your team, and even your organization's structure. Now we recommend that you turn that same understanding inward and understand your own limitations. Know them for what they are and respect them. In a modern organization, you can't last very long as a one-man band. Not even Tiger Woods plays in every golf tournament.

Once you've recognized your limitations, you can go about circumventing them. Sometimes this just means having an assistant you can trust to handle your travel arrangements and messaging, although, as Bill Ross observes, "In today's world of 'E-,' it's getting tougher to rely on other people. As the role of the assistant decreases, we increasingly have to leverage electronic and telecommunications tools for mundane tasks."

For problem solving, however, no one has yet devised a substitute for the human brain. Because you can't do everything yourself, you have to develop a group of people you can rely on to help you shoulder the burden. That group might be your official team or just an informal network you can call on for certain tasks. Once you've found people whose ability you trust, don't let them go—they're worth their weight in gold.

Depending on your position within the organization, you may not be able to delegate. Sewage, after all, flows downhill. In that case, you should become someone others can rely on. Eventually, you'll be able to move a bit upstream.

Make the most of your network. Beyond those in your inner circle whom you rely on, chances are you know a lot of other people with whom you share a set of experiences and values—a common culture. These people may be friends and acquaintances from earlier positions you held, fellow alumni from college or business school, or members of your church or synagogue. Wherever they come from, they are all part of your network, and they can help you get ahead, sometimes in surprising ways.

The network of McKinsey alumni is far closer than that of most other businesses—if anything, it resembles the alumni organization of a small college—and the Firm goes to great lengths to make it so. It might not surprise you to hear that a McKinsey associate in New York can leave a message for another McKinsey consultant in, say, Calcutta and expect a response within a day. What might surprise you is that a McKinsey alumnus can expect a similar level of response from other Firm alumni. This book is a prime example of that responsiveness. We could not have written it without the help of former McKinsey-ites who were willing to make time in their busy schedules for a couple of writers who, in many cases, they had never met before.

Chances are your current and former employers don't go to the same lengths as McKinsey in promoting their alumni organizations. Even so, you can build your own network. Stay in touch with your school alumni associations. Don't lose touch with former colleagues, clients, or even competitors. You never know where they'll turn up or when they might be in a position to help you.

Remember, too, that networking is a two-way street. If people help you or you want them to help you at some point, you have to be ready to help them when you can. Beyond that, make an effort to cast your bread upon the waters. If one day you get a call from, say, a younger alumnus of your alma mater, take the call and do what you can for him. Who knows, one day, that person may be in a position to help you.

YOUR PERSONAL LIFE

Life at McKinsey is a constant struggle between the professional and the personal. McKinsey consultants often work long hours, spend the entire workweek away from home, and come into the office on the weekend. They don't always get a chance to have dinner with their spouses, put their kids to bed, or just take a relaxing weekend to pore over the Sunday papers.

As a result, the ability to strike a balance between work and personal life becomes extremely important to one's success at the Firm. Not everyone manages it. Many of our alumni stated frankly that they left McKinsey because they couldn't strike that balance or didn't like the balance they had struck. Sometimes, what worked for single, twenty-something consultants stopped working when they became married, thirty-something parents.

Even so, our alumni learned several lessons (even if sometimes after the fact) about surviving the rigors of the high-pressure, executive life with one's sanity—and even one's marriage—intact.

Obviously, even more than the lessons on advancing one's career, these lessons will work for some and not for others. We offer them in the hope that they can help you.

THE McKINSEY WAY

McKinsey-ites often complain that they don't have time for a personal life. Even so, they had these two lessons on the subject.

Surviving on the road. Travel is part of modern business life. Try to see the opportunities in business travel, rather than the costs. If you're traveling someplace interesting, take advantage of it. If your destination is less than exotic, minimize the drudgery with proper planning. Pack light, make sure your transportation is reliably arranged, and find ways to entertain yourself when you stop working for the day. Don't let life on the road become an uninterrupted cycle of working, eating, and sleeping.

If you want a life, lay down some rules. When you work 80 hours or more per week, there's little time left over for anything else. If you want a life, you have to do a little advance work. Make one day a week off-limits. Keep work and home separate. Make plans when you know you'll have free time. Of course, sometimes events force you to violate your own rules. Still, because you laid down those rules in the first place, you and those around you—your boss, colleagues, spouse, kids—will know what to expect most of the time.

LESSONS LEARNED AND IMPLEMENTATION ILLUSTRATIONS

When you're on the fast track, you're busy, pulled in several directions at once, and can be under a lot of stress. To endure these pressures with your sanity intact, you have to be able to strike a balance between work and everything else. Clearly, one person's balance point will be another one's unendurable burden and someone else's half load. Wherever your balance point lies, the following lessons from McKinsey alumni will help you find it and stay on it:

- Respect your time.
- Perform sanity checks.
- Share the load.

Respect your time. Work is like a gas: it expands to fill the time available. This is certainly the case at McKinsey. In the New York office, one could easily log 100-hour weeks without stint yet still find more to do. Even in less entrepreneurial environments, like Europe, McKinsey puts heavy demands on its employees' time. As Heiner Kopperman, now with Change Works, joked, "At McKinsey's German offices, we liked the 35-hour workweek so much we did it twice a week."

When they leave the Firm, often in hopes of a better lifestyle, McKinsey alumni are sometimes surprised to find that this principle holds just as true for positions of responsibility in other organizations. One alumnus summed it up quite well: "Work never goes away. I come in at 6:00 every morning. I could stay until 8:00 every night and still not be finished." In his next sentence, however, he gives us the way out of this problem: "I could stay until 8:00 every night, but I choose not to. One thing I learned at McKinsey was that if things are not falling apart, just go at 5:00. Take advantage of the time."

You have to decide, based on your personal ambitions, the nature of your organization, and your place in the pecking order, how much of your time you will devote to work. The number itself matters only to you—it could be 40 hours per week or 90. Decide whether that includes one or both days of the weekend.

Working backward from that number, arrange your schedule accordingly. The start of your day is usually easiest to control: you know how long it usually takes you to get into the office and can set your alarm accordingly. The challenge comes at the end of the day; resist the temptation to tack on one more meeting or work that extra half hour. If you succumb, the meeting will drag on, and the half hour will become an hour. Before you know it, you're leaving the office at 10:00 every night.

You will also have to get others to respect your time. The better you are at your job or the higher up you go in your organization, the more everyone wants a piece of you. There's an old saying, "Stress is the feeling you get when your gut says, 'No,' and your mouth says, 'Yes, I'd be glad to.'" You have to train your mouth to say, "No." Learn to prioritize potential time commitments according to their ability to help you get things done. (You have to allow, of course, for drains on your time caused by political necessity. If your boss says you have to go to a meeting and you can't get him to change his mind, you're stuck.) You can also make your colleagues understand that you are a finite resource. Sometimes a little humor can help in this regard, as Leah Niederstadt discovered during her time at Reading Is Fundamental (RIF):

> My position was such that I became the clearinghouse for much of the information about our strategic plan. My phone rang constantly, and people were always knocking on my door for data that other people had. One day, a colleague gave me a dainty little wooden sign decorated with blue silk ribbons and bearing in delicately painted letters the words GO AWAY! My colleagues laughed when I hung it on my door, but the number of unnecessary interruptions decreased.

However you do it, making sure that those around you appreciate the value of your time will make you more productive and less harried by the end of the day.

Perform sanity checks. In life, as in business, sometimes you need to step back and look at the big picture. If your regular routine consists of leaving for the office before your kids wake up and seeing your spouse only when you crawl into bed at 1:00 a.m. after the Tokyo conference call, it might make sense to ask yourself a few pointed questions. Are you happy with your job? With your boss? With your organization? If not, then do the likely future rewards of your current situation justify the sacrifices you're making? If they don't, then are you really in the right position and/or career? If not, what should you do to change things? After working long hours, traveling constantly, and never seeing their families or even just the insides of their apartments, many McKinsey-ites ask themselves these questions. Often, the answers lead them to become McKinsey alumni.

Changing jobs is not the only answer, however, nor is it always an option. Sometimes you can manage the expectations of those around you—bring them closer to reality and reason—and improve your situation. If your spouse chafes at your workload, you need to demonstrate why what you're doing is worth the cost. If you can't do so convincingly, then why are you doing what you're doing? If your boss expects you to perform like Superman, you need to bring his expectations back to earth.

When work becomes an unreflective routine of long hours and constant demands, it's easy to lose sight of why you're doing what you're doing. Take a step back and look at the big picture, at what matters to you. After all, in the words of Socrates, "The unexamined life isn't worth living."

Share the load. When we wanted to find out how to balance the demands of work and family, we couldn't have asked a better person than Bob Garda. He spent 27 years at McKinsey and rose to become a director of the Firm and the head of the Firm's marketing practice. More important, he built a marriage and raised a family that survived the stresses of his demanding career both at McKinsey and after it. His secret:

> My wife. I have a very self-sufficient woman for a partner, and she really is a partner. We decided early on how to share the responsibilities of life. For instance, we figured out that she was a heck of a lot better than I was at dealing with contractors, such as plumbers and electricians, so she took care of all that. Other McKinsey partners handled this differently. As another example, I always discussed work and sought my wife's opinion and advice on client issues; she was an important behind-the-scenes team member. She was my best counselor and critic.
>
> I never second-guessed the decisions my wife made in my absence—I tried that once. I always supported her actions to show a united front to the children.

As Bob learned, achieving this kind of balance requires a commitment by both parties. Bob continues:

> Early on, we realized that personal time together, just the two of us, was important. After all, the children were going to be with us for only a short time in our married life. Thus, every year we'd take a week "honeymoon" that was tacked on to one of my business trips. We took advantage of the fact that grandparents love to baby-sit.

> Over a time, I also grew to understand that, when it comes to being with my family, it's not just "quality time" that matters, as I had been advised early on, but it's also "quantity time." Children want their questions answered now, not in three days when dad comes home. I could have spent all my time on work if I let myself, but I needed to be with my family. So I tried to manage my travel schedule to get home more often and kept weekends sacred. If I had to bring work home, I'd do it between 10 p.m. and 2 a.m., after everyone had gone to bed.

Bob knew, early in his career, that it's just as tough to be a one-man band at home as it is at the office. Having someone to share the load with can make all the difference.

What if you are single, unattached (whether by choice or by chance), or legally barred from entering into your preferred union? We've no wish to alienate anyone by talking exclusively about marriage. Though matrimony may be the most common way to share the burdens of life, it is by no means the only method—nor always the most successful. Friends and family can help share the load, too. If you rely on them to help you, remember that you owe them the same duty of honesty and reliability that you would a spouse.

Sharing the load means, first and foremost, being up-front about expectations. If you expect to work every weekend for the next five years, make sure your spouse knows it and is happy with it. If he's not, be prepared to compromise. Furthermore, once you make a commitment—"I won't work on weekends" or "I'll cook dinner three nights a week"—stick to it, barring life-and-death emergencies. If you seem to be having life-and-death emergencies every week (and you're not dealing with matters of real life and death, as in a trauma ward), take a hard look at your priorities.

You might want to bear in mind the words of Shyam Giridharadas, who left McKinsey to found Prism Consulting International: "I loved the Firm, but I was wedded to my family."

EXERCISES

We didn't see the point of exercises for this section. Life is for living, not for practice. Make the most of it.

CONCLUSION

In this chapter, even more so than in the rest of this book, we don't purport to have all the answers. We hope that you found at least something that can help you further your career and make your life a little better. If that's the case, then we've done our job.

One final point with regard to self-management: we believe that many people in the business world would benefit from lightening up a bit. Not that you shouldn't take yourself seriously. We're not advocating that everyone walk around with a sense of ironic detachment like the characters in "Seinfeld." We simply mean that there is, or ought to be, more to life than making the next sale or finishing the next report. As we said earlier in this chapter, it's important to maintain perspective, and having a life that extends beyond the confines of your office will help you in that regard.

* * *

We've now finished our journey through the McKinsey Mind. We hope that along the way you've learned something about how to improve your decision making, how to manage the decision-making process, and how to get your ideas across to your audience to help make change happen in your organization.

If there is one broad theme that connects all the elements of our model of the McKinsey Mind—analyzing, presenting, and managing—it is *truth*. The goal of problem solving is, after all, to uncover the truth and communicate it. That is how correct decisions get made and positive changes effected. But truth and the search for truth are more than mere tools that increase shareholder value. They are hallmarks of a free market and a free society, for without truth we cannot control our individual destinies nor generate the progress on which a dynamic society depends. As has been said since before the days of the ancient Greeks, when truth loses out to falsehood and superstition, freedom loses out to despotism and barbarism.

Even beyond that, however, truth carries an even higher significance. In the Talmud, the collection of rabbinic teachings on Jewish law written down some 1,800 years ago, the sage Simon ben Gamliel says, "Upon three things does the world rely: upon justice, upon truth, and upon harmony." And of these three, truth is the most important, for without truth there can be no justice, and a harmony based on falsehood will eventually collapse into acrimony and strife.

This last discussion has taken us a long way from problem-solving tools and management techniques. Compared to the preservation of a just and free society, improving the profitability of Acme Industry's thrum-mat division might seem like small potatoes. Maybe, but as individuals we have to start close to home, within our own spheres of action. Find the truth wherever you can, and the world will be a little bit better for it. We hope this book helps you in your quest.

Appendix A

DATA-GATHERING RESOURCES

Finding information about company, industry, or business topics can be a trying, even exasperating experience.* One reason for this is that no one source covers every aspect of every company, industry, or topic. You will likely have to look several places to find the information you want. Another reason for frustration is that some information is impossible or nearly impossible to find. This is particularly true for financial and structural information, as well as information about private companies and subsidiaries or divisions of larger companies.

While planning your research, you will want to ask yourself some questions:

- What is the correct corporate name?
- Is the company publicly held or privately held?

*Once again, our thanks to David Ernsthausen, information specialist at the Kenan-Flaglen School of Business at the University of North Carolina at Chapel Hill. Please note that, although these sources were correct at the time of writing, Web addresses and content can change rapidly.

- Is the company a subsidiary or division of another company?
- What information do I need to answer my questions?
- What indexes, databases, or other sources will contain this information?

Thousands of Internet sites, both free and fee-based, provide information about companies, industries, or business news. Choosing the sites that will work best for you will probably take some time and experimentation. No one site is *always* best for every information need. Also, remember that sometimes the best resource is not on the Internet at all but in printed form.

This Appendix offers a selected list of Internet sites and print resources that businesspeople may find useful for answering questions related to industries and companies. Your company library or information center may subscribe to some or all of these resources. You may also want to visit your local college, university, or public library to see what resources it has available to the general public.

JOURNAL AND NEWSPAPER ARTICLES

Articles from journals and newspapers can be a wonderful source of information about a company, an industry, business concepts, or the economy in general. You can use articles to gather information about a company or industry's history, its current activities, and sometimes its prospects for the future. Journal and newspaper articles can also be a good source of information about the economy in general, including worker shortages, credit availability, regulation, and other business-related issues. However, not every company and industry will generate much coverage in these periodicals.

The main way to find articles that have been published in newspapers and journals is to use an index. Table 3-1 in Chapter 3 lists several indexes that are particularly good for finding this kind of information. The most notable include ABI/Inform Global and Dow Jones Interactive. To use these indexes, you enter a word or phrase, and the search engine produces a list of citations and in many cases the full text of articles on the company, industry, or other subject.

If you are looking for stories about a smaller, perhaps regional company, you may want to start with the newspaper from the region or city where the company is located. *American Journalism Review's* AJR NewsLink website has a very good collection of links to more than 3,300 U.S. newspapers and business newspapers and more than 2,000 more from around the world. The dates covered vary from paper to paper; some go back to the mid-1990s.

INDUSTRY RESEARCH

The following lists identify selected Internet and print resources that may be helpful in researching particular industries.

ANALYST REPORTS

- *Investext*—This subscription service contains the full text of investment reports and forecasts for more than 11,000 U.S. and international companies and for 53 industries. The reports come from more than 520 brokerages, investment banks, and consulting firms around the world. For subscription information, go to www.tfsd.com/products/analyst/default.asp.

FINANCIAL AND PERFORMANCE RATIOS (INDUSTRY AVERAGES)

- *Almanac of Business and Industrial Financial Ratios*—This source contains tables of selected financial and operating ratios for more than 160 industries. There are 22 financial categories in 12 asset group sizes. Not all SIC codes are included in this work, so you may have to find an SIC code that is close to the one you are looking for. *Annual Statement Studies* and *Industry Norms and Key Business Ratios* are similar print resources from other publishers. You can find them in many university and public libraries.
- *Corporation Tax Statistics* (*www.irs.ustreas.gov/prod/tax_stats/soi/corp_id.html*)—This free site contains links to industry averages of information from corporate tax returns filed with the U.S. Internal Revenue Service. Data are drawn from corporate balance sheets, income statements, and other sources. Much of the most current data here are several years old.
- *Standard and Poor's Industry Surveys*—This print source is great for current descriptions of industries. Most industries are defined fairly broadly. Each description is around 30 pages long and includes some of the major current trends, a list of the major companies, and selected performance measures: financial statement information, financial and performance ratios for selected companies in the industry, and industry averages. This source also includes a useful section titled "How to Analyze a Company in this Industry." Another useful item is a short list of additional sources of industry information. This reference is available in many university and large public libraries.

INDUSTRY CLASSIFICATION CODES (SIC AND NAICS)

- *North American Industry Classification System* (www.census.gov/epcd/www/naics.html)—From the Census Department, the North American Industry Classification System (NAICS) provides common industry definitions for Canada, Mexico, and the United States. The NAICS is a joint effort of the U.S. Economic Classification Policy Committee, Statistics Canada, and Mexico's Instituto Nacional de Estadistica, Geografia e Informatica. With the goals of better comparing economic and financial statistics and ensuring that such statistics keep pace with the changing economy, the NAICS has begun to replace the countries' separate classification systems—including SIC codes in the United States—with one uniform system for classifying industries. This site does a good job of explaining the new system and provides information from government sources. One great feature of this site is the NAICS and SIC comparability table.

  There is also an unofficial NAICS site that pulls together information on NAICS, this time from government as well as nongovernment sources.
- *Standard Industrial Classification Search* (www.osha.gov/oshstats/sicser.html)—This resource allows the user to search the 1987 version of the SIC manual by keyword(s) to find a four-digit SIC code and to access descriptive information for a known four-digit SIC code.
- *North American Industry Classification System (NAICS)*—This printed resource contains detailed descriptions of what NAICS codes mean. It describes what types of companies are to be assigned which NAICS code.

INDUSTRY DESCRIPTIONS, OVERVIEWS, AND STATISTICS

- *Business.com* (www.business.com)—This site at first glance looks and feels very much like Yahoo, but it is totally dedicated to business information. It is organized by industry, and there is a directory of links to companies that provide products or services for the industry or subsections of the industry. After selecting an industry, if you scroll down to the "Industry Resources" section, you will find links called "Industry Basics" and "Industry Profile." Both of these links provide wonderful summary information for the industry selected.
- *Corporate Information* (www.corporateinformation.com)—Pull-down menus let you select from 30 industries and 65 countries to get a list of relevant links and a short write-up about the industry. You can also retrieve a list of companies that the site covers in that particular industry and reports on some (but not all) of the companies in the industry.
- *Current Industrial Reports* (www.census.gov/ftp/pub/cir/www)—These annual and quarterly reports from the U.S. Census Bureau contain a variety of statistics on industries in the United States, including lists of companies in an industry.
- *Encyclopedia of American Industries*—This set contains brief (three- to four-page) descriptions of industries, organized by SIC codes. Each entry includes a brief description of the industry, the workforce, the organization and structure, the current conditions, the industry leaders, and—perhaps most important—a list of selected additional readings. This encyclopedia is available at many university libraries and large public libraries.

- *Industry Reference Handbooks*—This seven-volume set contains overviews, descriptions, and statistics for a wide variety of industries. The seven volumes are titled *Computers & Software, Pharmaceuticals, Telecommunications, Chemicals, Health & Medical Services, Hospitality*, and *Entertainment*. This set is available in many university libraries and large public libraries.
- *Office of Trade and Economic Analysis* (www.ita.doc.gov/td/industry/otea)—As the website says, this office of the Department of Commerce conducts a "comprehensive program of data development, dissemination, and research and analysis on international and domestic trade and investment issues to support trade promotion and trade policy responsibilities of Trade Development, International Trade Administration Department of Commerce, and United States Government organizations and officials. The office also coordinates the trade policy implementation activities of the Trade Development unit." The website provides links to a variety of foreign trade, investment, and industry statistics.
- *Standard and Poor's Industry Surveys*—This print source is great for current descriptions of industries. Most industries are defined rather broadly. Each description is around 30 pages long and includes some major current trends, a list of the major companies, and selected financial information (data from financial statements, financial and performance ratios for selected companies in the industry, and industry averages). This source also includes a useful section titled "How to Analyze a Company in this Industry." Another useful item is a short list of additional sources of industry information. This source is available in many university libraries and large public libraries.

- *TableBase* (www.galegroup.com/welcome.html)—This subscription service allows you to search for information that appeared in tables and charts of journal articles. Information found may include summary statistics about companies, industries, products, markets, and consumer behavior, including rankings, forecasts, market shares, and product sales.
- *U.S. Industry & Trade Outlook*—This source contains short (two- to five-page) synopses of broad trends and forecasts for various industries in the United States. For each industry, there is also a short reading list for those who would like more information on the industry.

MAJOR COMPETITORS

- *Business Rankings Annual*—This source is a collection of tables and charts ranking companies within various industries by measures that have appeared in articles in several journals. There is not necessarily a chart or table for every industry. Most of the data in the current volume are at least a year or two old.
- *Current Industrial Reports* (www.census.gov/ftp/pub/cir/www)—These annual and quarterly reports from the U.S. Census Bureau contain a variety of statistics on industries in the United States, including lists of companies in an industry.
- *Hoover's Online* (www.hoovers.com)—This service provides some free and some subscription information. Basic directory and financial information on more than 13,500 public and private companies is available for free. If you subscribe, you can get in-depth profiles of some 3,400 public and private companies in the United States and around

the world. Hoover's also publishes several print resources. Two of the more interesting are *Hoover's Handbook of Emerging Companies* and *Hoover's Handbook of Private Companies*.

- *Standard & Poor's Register of Corporations*—This is a wonderful four-volume print resource for finding addresses, telephone numbers, and names of executives for corporations. For some of the executives, there is a short biographical sketch. These books are available in many university libraries and large public libraries.
- *Thomas Register of American Manufacturers* (www.thomasregister.com)—This free Internet resource lets you look up a product, service, or brand name and find directory-style listings for companies that manufacture or supply it. You can also look up a company name to find lists of the products or services that company can provide. However, this is not an exhaustive listing of companies or products. Company listings typically include addresses and phone numbers as well as products available. This resource is free, but you must register to use it.

RANKINGS AND RATINGS

- *American Tally Statistics & Rankings for 3,165 U.S. Cities*—This reference provides demographic, sociological, and economic statistics on a large cross-section of American cities. Not every city is included in every table or chart. This source is available at many public and university libraries.
- *Business Rankings Annual*—This source is a collection of tables and charts ranking companies within various industries by measures that have appeared in journal articles.

There is not necessarily a chart or table for every industry. Most of the data in the current volume are at least a year or two old.

- *Gale State Rankings Reporter*—This resource allows you to check how the states stack up on a variety of demographic, sociological, and economic measures. This source is available at many public and university libraries.
- *Market Share Reporter*—This source is a collection of tables and charts that depict market share for all kinds of products and services that have appeared in articles in various journals. There is not necessarily a chart or table for every product or service. Most of the data in the current volume are at least a year or two old.
- *Price's List of Lists* (gwis2.circ.gwu.edu/~gprice/listof.htm)—This site has links to a wide range of lists and rankings. Here is a description in the designers' own words: "The Internet contains numerous lists of information. Many of these lists present information in the form of rankings of different people, organizations, companies, etc. This collection is designed to be a clearinghouse for these types of resources. Hopefully, it will allow these useful tools to be located and accessed in a timely and efficient manner. Many of these lists have been designed to be interactive/searchable and provide greater utility than the printed versions."
- *World Market Share Reporter*—This source, much like *Market Share Reporter*, is a collection of tables and charts that depict market share for all kinds of products and services mentioned in various journals, except the focus is on worldwide or non-U.S. rankings and shares. There is not necessarily a chart or table for every product or service. Most of the data in the current volume are at least a year or two old.

COMPANY INFORMATION

Current financial, directory, and historical information on companies also appears in a number of electronic sources, including the company's annual report and corporate website. The information available on any given company will depend on the type of database or print resource you are using, the size of the company, and whether the company is public, private, or a subsidiary. Generally speaking, large companies whose stock is publicly traded are easiest to find more information on; conversely, smaller private companies are typically hardest to find information on. For smaller or private companies, a newspaper or journal article may be a more fruitful source of information.

DIRECTORIES

- *Companies Online* (www.companiesonline.com)—This site offers basic directory information (address, telephone number, and perhaps names of a few top officers) for over 900,000 public and private companies.
- *CorpTech Directory of Technology Companies*—This directory focuses on high-tech companies. Each listing typically contains the company's mailing address, telephone number, names of top executives, the year the company was founded, a list of SIC codes, a sales estimate, and a brief description of what the company does. Check for this print resource at your local university library.
- *Million Dollar Directory*—This source is good for finding addresses, telephone numbers, and names of the top officers of major corporations. This print resource is available in the collections of many university libraries and large public libraries.

- *Standard & Poor's Register of Corporations*—This is a wonderful print resource for finding corporations' addresses, telephone numbers, and names of executives. For some of the executives, there are short biographical sketches. This four-volume reference is available at many university libraries and large public libraries.
- *Thomas Register of American Manufacturers* (www.thomasregister.com)—This free Internet resource lets you look up a product, service, or brand name and find directory-style listings for companies that manufacture or supply it. You can also look up a company name to find lists of the products or services that company can provide. This is not an exhaustive listing of companies or products. Company listings typically include addresses, phone numbers, and products available. This resource is free, but you must register to use it.

COMPANY DESCRIPTIONS, OVERVIEWS, AND FINANCIAL AND OTHER STATISTICS

- *Corporate Affiliations Plus*—This database is available in a variety of electronic formats, including CD-ROM. It contains descriptive and financial data on approximately 16,000 major domestic and foreign corporations and their 140,000 subsidiaries, divisions, and affiliates. It covers companies traded on the New York and American stock exchanges, companies with affiliates that are traded over the counter, and major private companies and their affiliates. The information provided includes name, address, telephone number, stock exchange, ticker symbol, SIC codes, business description, corporate hierarchy (when available), key personnel, directors, net worth, total assets, and total liabilities. The database corresponds to three print resources that may be held by many university or public libraries: the *Directory of Corporate Affiliations*, the *International Directory of Corporate Affiliations*, and the *Directory of Leading Private Companies*.

- *Corporate Information* (www.corporateinformation.com)—This website lets you type in a ticker symbol or company name and retrieve a report on any of more than 20,000 companies. Pull-down menus also let you select from 30 industries and 65 countries to get a list of relevant links and a short write-up about the industry. You can also retrieve a list of companies that the site covers in that particular industry, as well as reports on some but not all of the companies in the industry.
- *FIS On-Line Global Data Direct* (www.fisonline.com)—This subscription service provides information on approximately 20,000 companies from about 80 countries. Data include brief company histories, business, property, officers, directors, long-term debt, Moody's ratings, capital stock, income statement, balance sheet, stock splits, and dividend payment history.
- *Hemscott.net* (www.hemscott.com)—This excellent site for business news is based in and focuses on Great Britain. You can find financial news, information on British companies, and prices for stocks traded on British exchanges. You must register, but most of the information is free.
- *Hoover's Online* (www.hoovers.com)—This service offers some free and some subscription information. Basic directory and financial information on more than 13,500 public and private companies is available for free. If you subscribe, you can get in-depth profiles of some 3,400 public and private companies in the United States and around the

world. Hoover's also publishes several print resources that focus on particular types of companies. Two of the more interesting print resources are *Hoover's Handbook of Emerging Companies* and *Hoover's Handbook of Private Companies*.

- *International Directory of Company Histories*—This multivolume set contains short to medium-length (two- to ten-page) narratives on the history of companies. Many of the histories include a bibliography of other places to look for information on the company discussed in the entry. At 33 volumes and counting, this print resource is in the collections of many university libraries and large public libraries.
- *Moody's Manuals*—There are several different *Moody's Manuals*. Each contains descriptions of companies in a broadly defined category: Bank and Finance, Industrials, Transportation, Utilities, and OTC Industrials. Company descriptions typically include address, officers, subsidiaries, technical information about any outstanding debt and stock, and abbreviated financial statements for several years. These volumes are a print counterpart to the electronic database Global Data Direct, listed earlier. Because many academic libraries have back issues of the *Moody's Manuals*, these references are particularly useful if you are looking for information that is more than a few years old.
- *Stock Research Sites on the Web* (depts.washington.edu/balib/stocksites)—There are hundreds of Internet sites that contain information relating to a company's stock. The trouble is finding a site that has the stock information that you are looking for. The librarians at the Foster Business Library at the University of Washington have put together this page to help solve this problem. Use this site to check which of 65 stock research sites have the information you

are looking for. The List of Sites Evaluated, the Comparative Evaluation, and the Screen for Sites are particularly useful.

- *TableBase* (www.galegroup.com/welcome.html)—This subscription service allows you to search for information that appeared in tables and charts of journal articles. Information found may include summary statistics about companies, industries, products, markets, and consumer behavior, including rankings, forecasts, market shares, and product sales.
- *Value Line Investment Survey (Expanded Edition)*—This is a good source for general information on public companies. Each entry typically contains a very brief history, abbreviated financial figures, a few financial and performance ratios, a chart of stock prices over a three-year period, a beta for the firm's stock, and a "timeliness" measure for the company's industry. *Value Line* is updated on a rotating basis, so each company is updated about once every 13 weeks or so. *Value Line* is in the collections of most university libraries and large public libraries.

REPORTS BY ANALYSTS OR THE COMPANY ITSELF

- *Academic Universe* (www.lexis-nexis.com)—Lexis-Nexis developed this database for the academic market. It provides links to general, regional, and international news, as well as to company news and financial information. To find information about a specific company, click on "Business," then on "Company Financial," then "Compare Companies," "SEC Filings & Reports," or one of the other links. Most of the time, the full text of the information is available. Lexis-Nexis has a variety of other products that they sell to corporate customers.

- *EDGAR* (www.sec.gov/edgarhp.htm)—This Internet site from the Securities and Exchange Commission provides access to the full text of 10-K reports, proxies, and other reports that publicly traded companies must file with the SEC.
- *Investext* (www.tfsd.com/products/analyst/default.asp)—This subscription service contains the full text of investment reports and forecasts for more than 11,000 U.S. and international companies and for 53 industries. The reports come from more than 520 brokerages, investment banks, and consulting firms around the world.
- *Report Gallery* (www.reportgallery.com)—This site provides access to more than 2,200 corporate annual reports plus "Zack's Snapshots," a report of earnings estimates, buy-sell-hold recommendations, and each company's rank in its industry.

OTHER RESOURCES: GUIDES TO FINDING INFORMATION

Many companies and university libraries have guides to business research available on their websites. These websites can be valuable tools for conducting business research. The following list represents just a few of the sites that are out there.

- *Baker Library Industry information Guides* (www.library.hbs.edu/industry/aboutguides.htm)—This wonderful set of 13 or so guides prepared by the librarians of the Baker

Library at Harvard Business School advises users on where to get information about a specific industry. The guides are written for Harvard students and faculty, but many of the resources mentioned will be available in other libraries.

- *Cole Library of Rensselaer at Hartford* (www.rh.edu/library/industry/industry.htm)—This is another set of guides on how to find information on specific industries. It lists a few more industries than at the Harvard website, but there seem to be fewer sources listed per industry.
- *Fuld & Co. Internet Intelligence Index* (www.fuld.com/i3/index.html)—Fuld & Co. is one of the premier competitive intelligence companies in the United States and perhaps the world. Its Internet Intelligence Index is a resource for gathering intelligence about competitors. According to this website, the index "contains links to over 600 intelligence-related Internet sites, covering everything from macro-economic data to individual patent and stock quote information."

Appendix B

LESSONS FROM *THE McKINSEY WAY*

At the beginning of each section of this book, we summarize the relevant lessons from *The McKinsey Way* (*TMW*). This Appendix is simply a list of where lessons from *TMW* appear in *The McKinsey Mind*. Those of you who want to follow up on your favorite lessons from *TMW* can use the table below to show you where to turn in this book.

Chapter 1. Framing the Problem

Feel free to be MECE 3

Don't reinvent the wheel (Part 1) 3

Solve the problem at the first meeting—the initial hypothesis 15

The problem is not always the problem 17

Chapter 2. Designing the Analysis

Find the key drivers 33

Look at the big picture 33

Don't boil the ocean 34

Sometimes you have to let the solution come to you 34

Chapter 3. Gathering the Data

Facts are friendly 52
Don't accept "I have no idea" 52
Specific research tips 52
Be prepared: write an interview guide 61
When conducting interviews, listen and guide 61
Seven tips for successful interviews 62
Don't leave the interviewee naked 62
Difficult interviews 63
Always write a thank-you note 63
Don't reinvent the wheel (Part 2) 76

Chapter 4. Interpreting the Results

80/20 86
Make a chart every day 86
Don't make the facts fit your solution 87
Make sure the solution fits your client 95

Chapter 5. Presenting Your Ideas

Be structured 105
The elevator test 105
KIS—one message per chart 105
Pre-wire everything 117
Tailor your presentation to your audience 121

Chapter 6. Managing Your Team

Getting the mix right 129
Recruiting McKinsey style 129
Keep the information flowing 137
Take your team's temperature to maintain morale 143
A little team bonding goes a long way 143

Chapter 7. Managing Your Client

How to sell without selling 160
Be careful what you promise: structuring an engagement 161
Engage the client in the process 165

[illegible] over your shoulder [illegible]
[illegible] the client is on your side [illegible]
[illegible] with [illegible] client [illegible] 165
[illegible]
[illegible]
[illegible]
[illegible]
[illegible]
[illegible]
[illegible]
[illegible]
[illegible]
[illegible] down [illegible] 176

Appendix C

IMPLEMENTATION LESSONS

The McKinsey Mind focuses on implementing McKinsey tools and techniques in other organizations. For quick reference and to help you address specific issues in your own company, we provide the following list of these new implementation lessons along with their locations in the main text.

INDEX